the POT *the* VESSEL *the* OBJECT

Fifty years of change and diversity in the Craft Potters Association

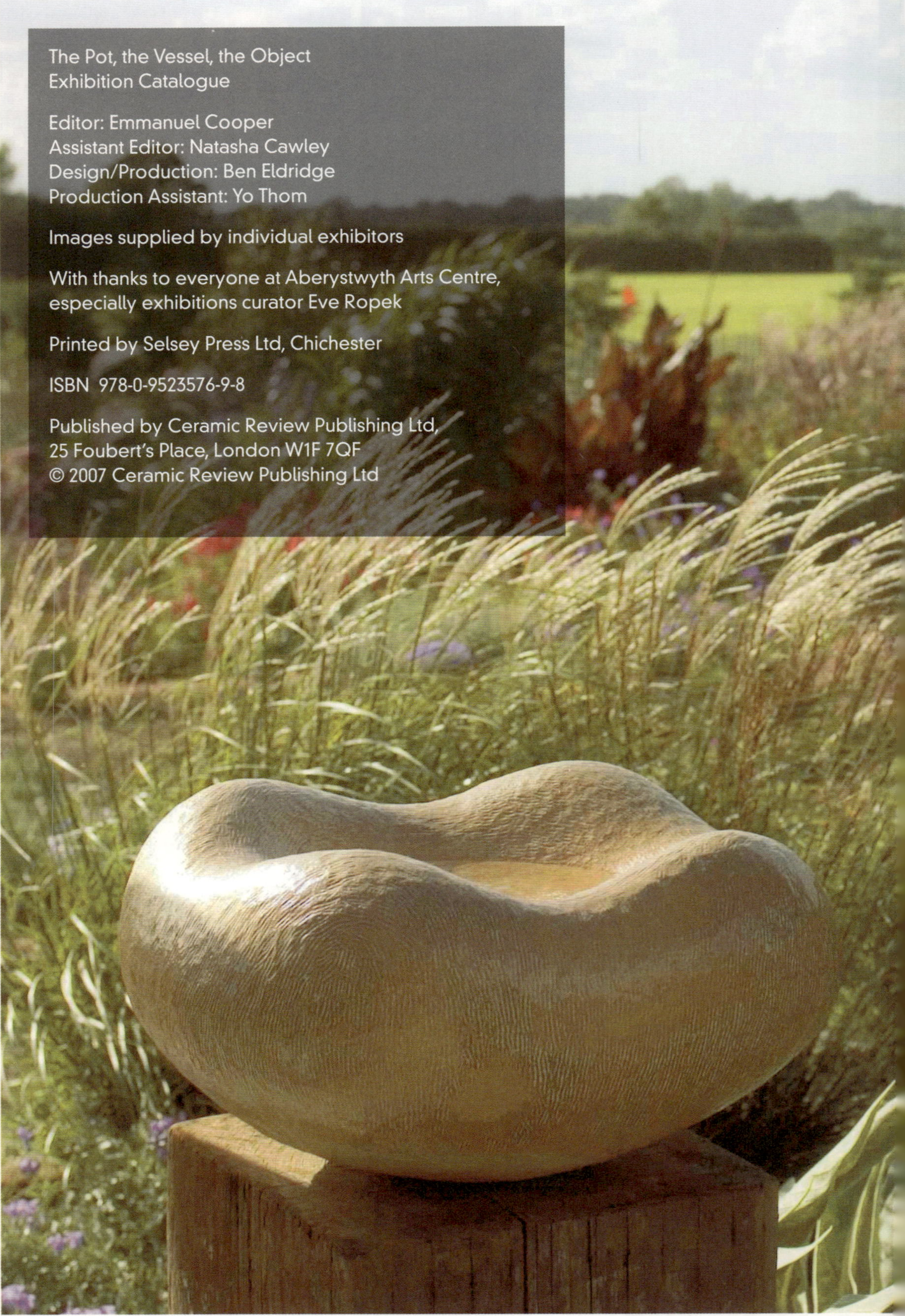

The Pot, the Vessel, the Object
Exhibition Catalogue

Editor: Emmanuel Cooper
Assistant Editor: Natasha Cawley
Design/Production: Ben Eldridge
Production Assistant: Yo Thom

Images supplied by individual exhibitors

With thanks to everyone at Aberystwyth Arts Centre, especially exhibitions curator Eve Ropek

Printed by Selsey Press Ltd, Chichester

ISBN 978-0-9523576-9-8

Published by Ceramic Review Publishing Ltd,
25 Foubert's Place, London W1F 7QF

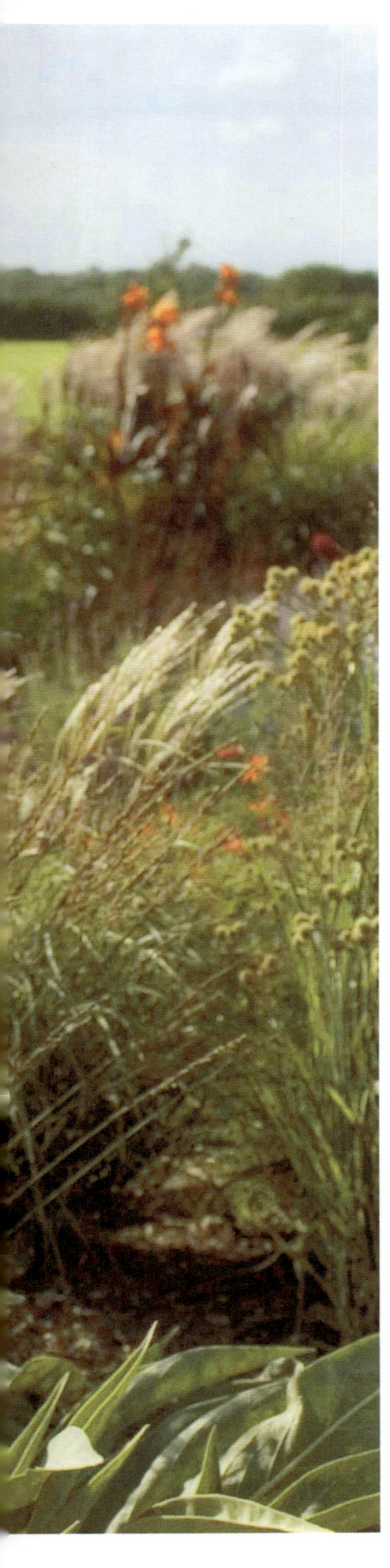

CONTENTS

INTRODUCTION

The Craft Potters Association (CPA) has a remarkable history. Founded as the result of a series of meetings and consultations which took place during 1957, The Craftsmen Potters Association, as it was first known, was launched as an Industrial and Provident Society early in the following year. Its development over the past fifty years is chronicled here in the catalogue essays written by some of the people who have been influential during its formative years. Guided by its elected Council, the CPA has, unlike some other crafts organisations, steered a steady course. Financially independent and democratically governed, it has, through thick and thin, supported its membership in practical ways and done much to educate and expand the audience for contemporary work. Despite limited financial resources – it has to earn what it spends – the CPA has never been afraid to take the initiative and to find new ways of strengthening the position of ceramic artists in our changing society.

The Pot, the Vessel, the Object is an exhibition which is anchored soundly in the present. The days when the entire CPA membership could take part in an exhibition like this are long past. To have to choose some forty makers from an exhibiting membership of three hundred is a difficult task and I regret that so many fine artists could not be included. However, I believe that the exhibition will provide an opportunity to see some of the best work being produced today. It will also be a place to assess the way that studio ceramics has developed, to see also the contemporary face of the CPA and to place the association within the contemporary crafts world.

Any major anniversary is a point in time for reflection and reassessment; it should also inspire and illuminate a way into the future. The next stage in the life of the CPA is certain to be challenging, but it will also be exciting. The Council and membership will have to deal with major issues affecting how the association will function. How can we further develop our support for members, how can we continue to expand interest in studio ceramics, how can we use technology to communicate better, how will we continue to flourish in a harsh commercial world? These questions and many more must be dealt with. With the collective experience of its first fifty years, I know that the CPA will continue to be a vibrant force in British ceramics.

Jack Doherty, Chair, Craft Potters Association

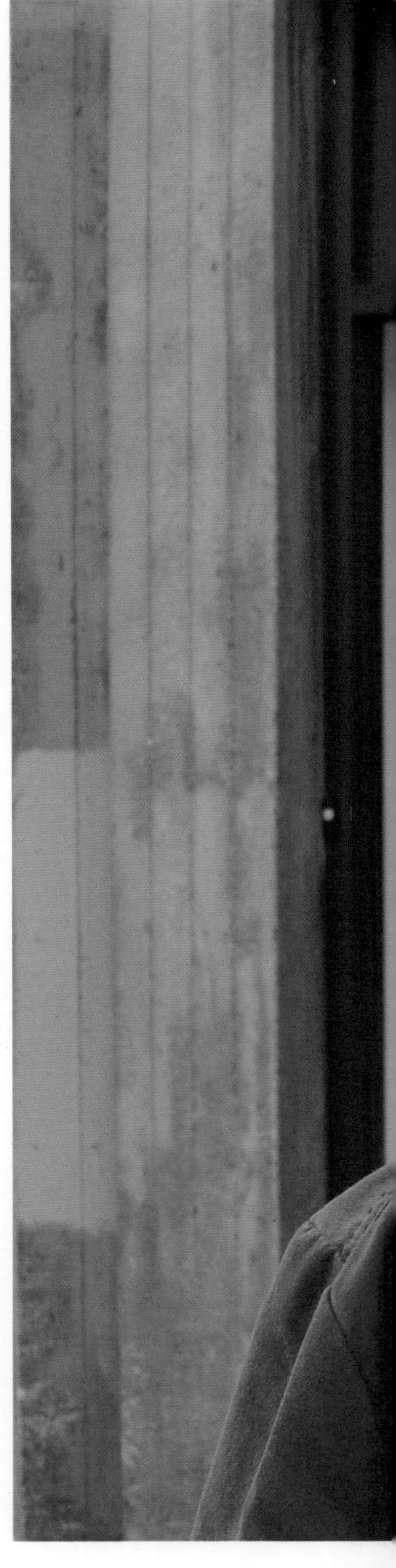

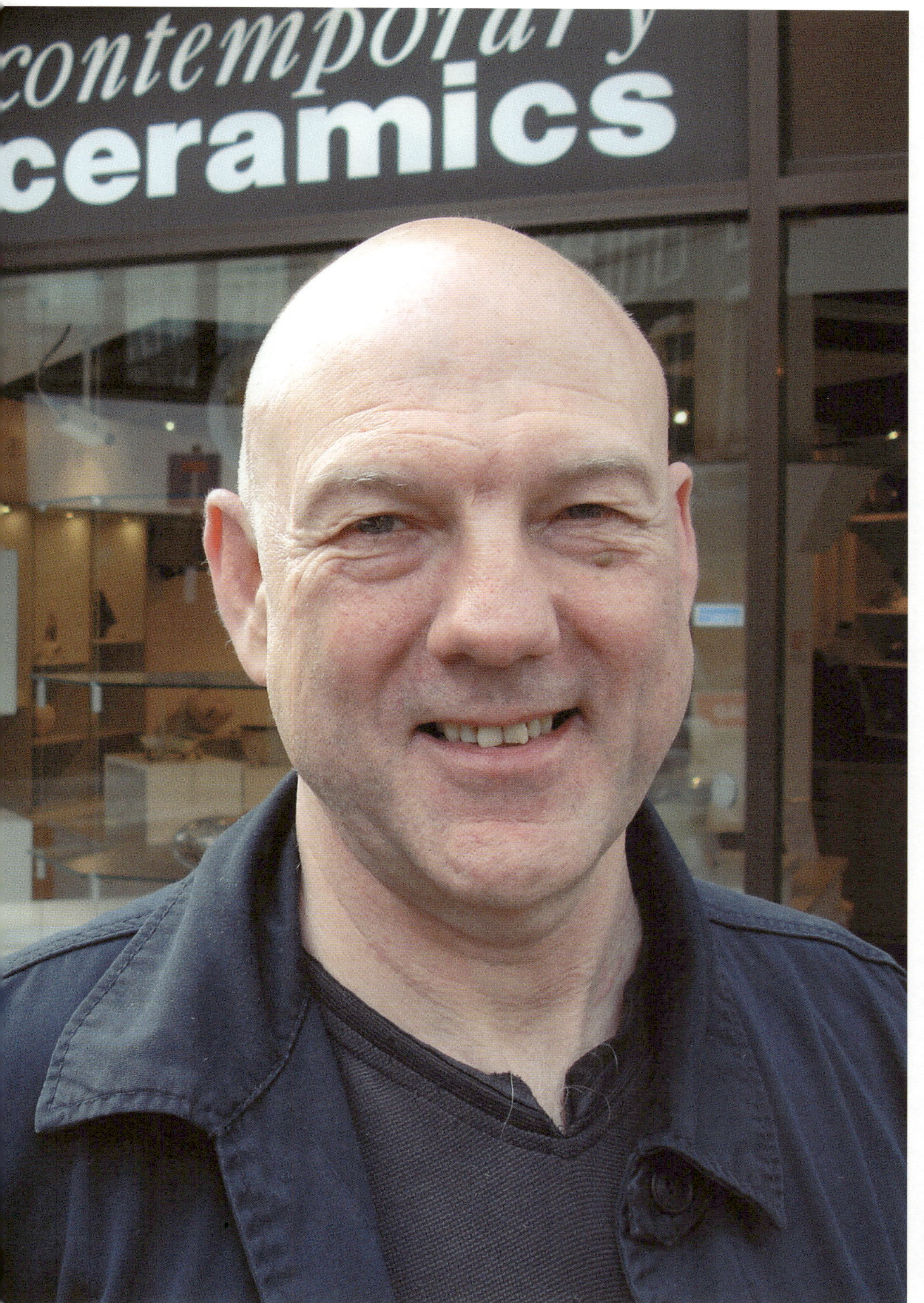
contemporary
ceramics

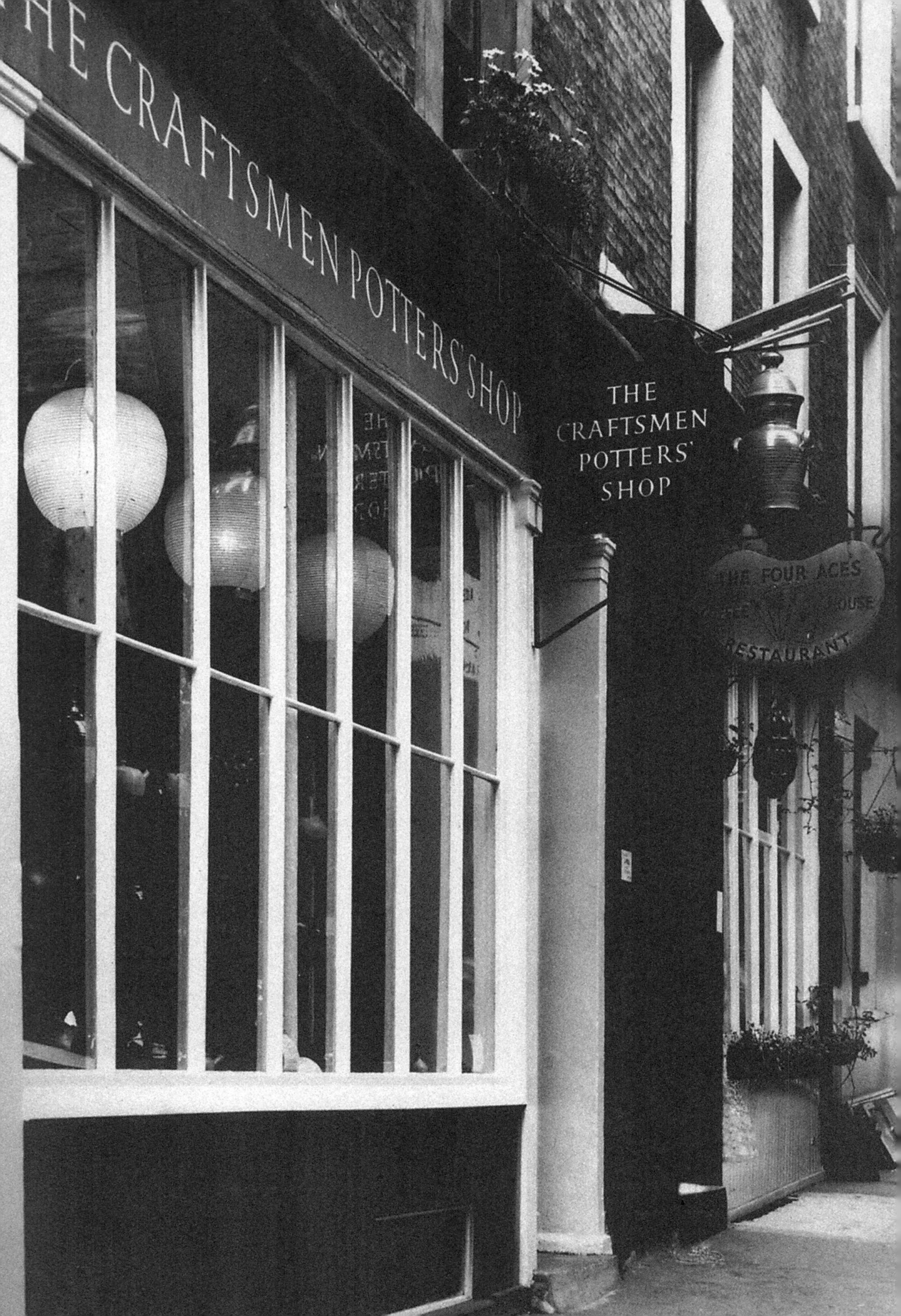
THE CRAFTSMEN POTTERS' SHOP
THE
CRAFTSMEN
POTTERS'
SHOP
THE FOUR ACES
RESTAURANT

THE EARLY YEARS

by Rosemary Wren

"Thirty-eight potters came to the initial meeting; none of us could previously have met so many kindred spirits at once before"

◁ The outside of the Craftsmen Potters Shop, 3 Lowndes Court, London, a pot by Denise Wren forming part of the sign

▽ Rosemary Wren (left) and Denise Wren (Photo courtesy Rosemary Wren)

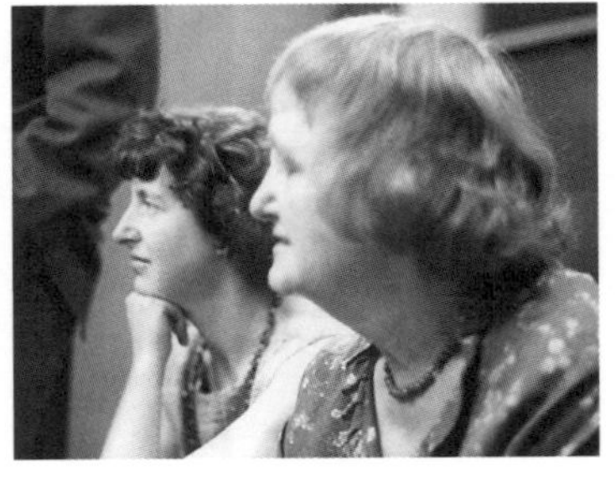

Few people can imagine all the hard thinking, energy, enthusiasm and sheer slogging work involved in the days when the Craftsmen Potters Association (CPA) was young. To clarify my version I have chased events through the hoarded papers now before me. Here then is the start: 'Minutes of the Meeting of Potters on 25 July 1956, in connection with the Export Display at the Rural Industries Bureau'.

The imposition of Purchase Tax on 'household goods' was causing problems to which exporting – under licence – was the theoretical answer, and Walter Lipton, Marketing Officer of the Rural Industries Bureau (RIB), an organisation that promoted mostly small rural industries, set up a meeting of potters to discuss ways to help. Thirty-eight potters came to the initial meeting; none of us could previously have met so many kindred spirits at once before. An exhibition of pots was arranged at the headquarters of the RIB in Wimbledon, which attracted visits from thirty overseas buyers. The entire exhibition was sold to a New Zealand store, and a repeat asked for in South Africa. A potential market undoubtedly existed in many countries, but the RIB could only pioneer. It was up to potters to form an association that could organise a permanent display of our work and export as a group.

The minutes of the meeting that follow show a mood of developing exhilaration. A modest display of samples was soon left far behind – the

▷ View of the exhibition organised by the Rural Industries Bureau at its headquarters in Wimbledon in 1956.

▽ Top picture – left: Rosemary Wren, centre: Denis Moore. Bottom picture – Walter Lipton is to the right with his arms folded

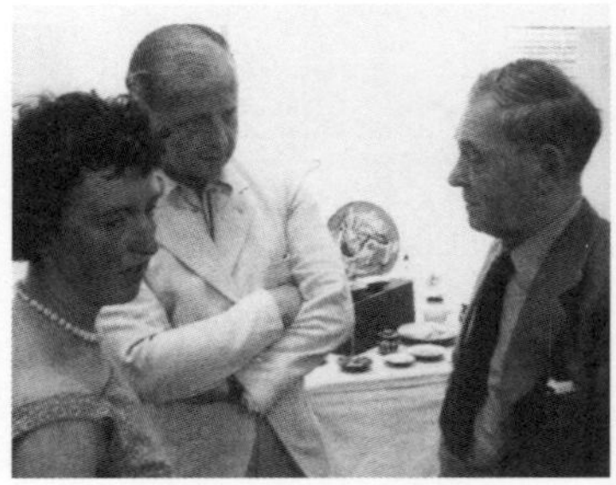

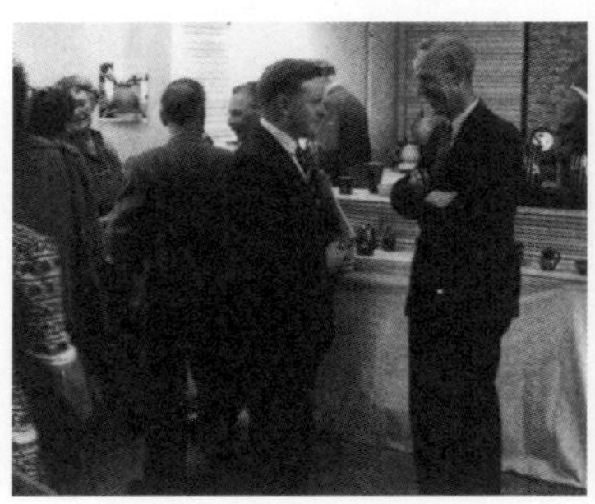

most vocal potters were individualists who did not work to sample anyway. Everyone wanted a proper Potters' Centre in London but the obvious problem was finance. A Working Party of nine was appointed to deliberate, investigate and prepare a detailed report.

A POTTERS' CO-OPERATIVE

The range of potters involved in the early planning is instructive in its combination of small scale producers and individual studio potters. Mr F J Watson of Wattisfield was a third-generation flowerpot maker with thirty employees. Keith Corrigan ran the pottery at Holkham Hall with seventeen employees. Reg Southcliffe's workshop made Welsh lustre ware at Cregiau, Cardiff. Ray Marshall worked in partnership in Sussex. Denis Moore (Surrey) and Roger Ross Turner (Dorset) each had one helper, Helen Pincombe (Surrey) worked alone, I worked separately from my mother, Denise Wren, though together we formed The Oxshott Pottery. Our first meeting was on 24 September 1956, secretarial help and a meeting room being provided at first by the RIB.

Walter Lipton's assistance was invaluable. He revealed that he had helped the furniture makers to start a similar association, the most suitable form being a non profit-sharing Industrial and Provident Society on the democratic lines laid down by Act of Parliament in 1893. We would have only to decide the Name and Objects of the Association, who should be the members and associates, and how the Council should be comprised. It sounded straightforward – but anyone knowing potters and the individuals concerned in particular would know that it was not.

The name was agreed easily. The term 'craftsmen' implied a high standard of skill and background knowledge, while the term 'Craftsmen Potters' was then seen to refer to both men and women. It also distinguished us from industrial potters. Each of us contributed something different to the 'Objects'. Roger Ross Turner's letter pleaded that each potter's technical research should be available to all – a generosity of approach that became part of the ethos of the CPA. Denis Moore was concerned about individual liberty and high standards, but deplored the eventual typography of the Rules; Keith Corrigan and Reg Southcliffe were business-like in their suggestions for the importance of increasing sales and handling problems collectively. Mr Watson was amazed at our verbosity; we respected him as the only truly traditional potter in the group. Those representing

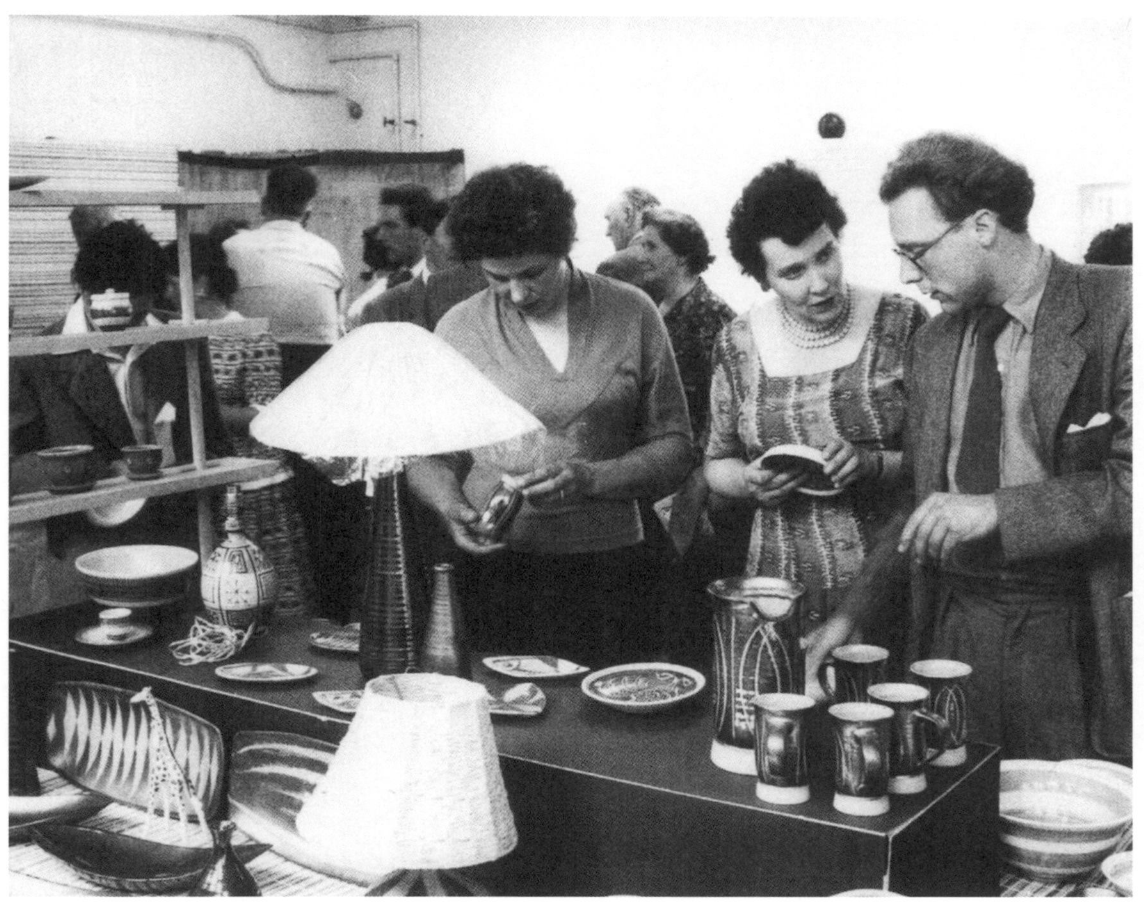

"The name was agreed easily. The term 'craftsmen' implied a high standard of skill and background knowledge, while the term 'Craftsmen Potters' was then seen to refer to both men and women"

smaller workshops wanted to ensure that 'work of original design and individual character' would not be overwhelmed by larger production potteries. I hoped we could make a society that everyone could feel to be a channel for sharing their own particular interests.

Defining the membership was thorny. The intention was to encourage technical freedom used with professional standards, so the first application form stated that membership was open to all individuals or groups 'possessing kilns and workshops and selling their pots to the public under an individual mark'. The Rules, however give the Council absolute discretion although only a General Meeting can expel a member. With a Working Party of such diversity the 'principle of non-selection' was inevitable; the Objects were to benefit all, not a selected few.

Denise Wren, my mother, was invited to the last meeting before the publication of the Report. Although asked to join the Working Party she had preferred to stay in the background contributing ideas and enthusiastic support; in appreciation she was later made an honorary member on her 80th birthday in 1971. Bernard Leach was also invited to give his views; he however felt that without selection unworthy work would be promoted. Eventually he accepted honorary membership after 1961, when the greatly increased number of pots and potters forced the reluctant decision that our Objects would be better served by a selected membership. Finally, it was laid down that the Council members should represent workshops of various sizes and regions. We were determined not to be run by a clique.

Our report complete, an Open Meeting was held at 6 Queen Square, Bloomsbury, London, on Saturday, 16 February 1957. The Working Party appointed a provisional Council with the addition of a town potter, Eileen Lewenstein of Briglin Pottery. By May a banking account had been opened and subscriptions could be received: for individual potters, £3.3s.0d, for Associates £1.1s.0d, for students 7s.6d. In August, when the first Newsletter was sent out, there were already fifty members and ten associates, Lady Leicester who owned Holkham Pottery, Norfolk, had become the first Vice-President, Reg Southcliffe and I were Vice-Chairmen, taking the meetings alternately. Five small exhibitions were arranged – at Blakeney in Norfolk, at Holkham, at Briglin Pottery (then at 66 Baker Street, London) with a parallel display at Heal's, Tottenham Court Road, London, and at Cregiau, Cardiff. Newsletter No. 2 reports great interest at all these exhibitions. Thanks to Briglin Pottery we had made our London debut and articles had appeared in *Vogue*, the *Manchester Guardian* and *Pottery Gazette*.

On 22 February 1958, the Foundation Meeting of 120 people took place at the Royal Hotel, Russell Square, London. The Rules had at last been signed by us and officially registered. Denis Moore gave a Progress Report and, since a body of members now existed, a council could be elected, the original Working Party/Provisional Council being asked to carry on. Michael Cardew, then Associate No. 7, working overseas, later our first honorary member, gave a 'scintillating address'.

Newsletter No. 3 (April 1958) announced that the CPA now has its own honorary secretary, the Council having appointed David Canter. Living near Oxshott, he had been coming to my evening classes; hearing from me about the CPA's urgent need for an organising secretary he wondered if this was something he could do to help. Apparently he went to the Foundation Meeting, then on my copy of the agenda for the following Council Meeting on 26 March 1958, at Caxton Hall is a pencilled arrow between items 3. 'Matters Arising' and 4. 'Premises' with the scribbled insertion 'David Canter'. We had thought we were just trying him out on the summer exhibitions; but thus began a loyal connection, arduous and fruitful, that continued for the rest of his life.

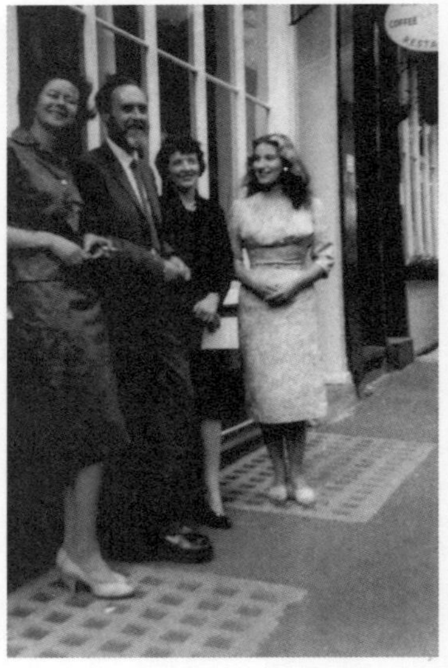

"David Canter's first Newsletter describes how he scoured Soho for potato baskets in which to transport the pots, eventually staggering up Regent Street balancing stacks of them on his head"

◁ Outside 3 Lowndes Court during a Ray Finch stoneware exhibition, 1960. Left to right: Anita Hoy, Ray Finch, Eileen Lewenstein, Pan Henry

▽ Pan Henry and David Canter in the Craftsmen Potters Shop, 3 Lowndes Court

On the way to that meeting David Canter and I had visited Pamela, Lady Glenconner in Notting Hill Gate who had offered her beautiful turquoise drawing room for a London exhibition. Immediately she became a firm friend of the CPA and became President for many years. Her sympathy, charm and tact were unfailing and, combined with the subtly appropriate wit of her literary quotations, have made many an occasion sparkle.

Within a week David Canter was sweeping those of us who lived near London along on the tide of his organisational energy. Three Summer Exhibitions were put together as one transportable Travelling Exhibition. David's first Newsletter (No. 4, July 1958) describes how he scoured Soho for potato baskets in which to transport the pots, eventually staggering up Regent Street balancing stacks of them on his head. 700 pots were entered from forty-five members. An impressive 510 pots were eventually sold for a total of £307. Elegant gilt-edged cards were printed for the Glenconner show. The Council, though shocked at the price, accepted that only the best was good enough. The cost of this was balanced by frugality in other areas and the hard work of an enthusiastic band of helpers. My mother arranged the exhibits. Pamela herself 'was tireless in her conducted tours' and came to know everyone's work and background. The accounts give the cost of the whole series as £183.12s.3d.

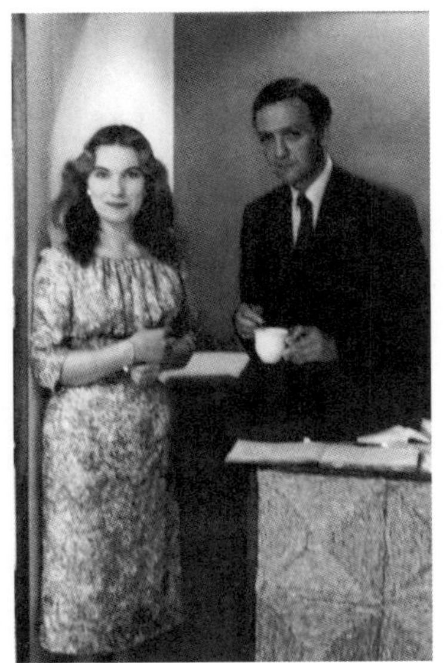

THE SHOP

In the file marked Premises, dated 10 March 1958, a tentative plan was discussed for running our own shop. Meanwhile ideas were simmering for a Potters Day, suited to members of all sorts. It materialised at Oxshott on 12 October 1958 when 103 visitors examined our new saltglaze kiln, watched Mr Nixon of Wrecclesham throwing flowerpots and Mr Bateson of Ambleside throwing big pots; there was a visit to a collection of Persian pots – and at Pinewoods nearby talking, mixing and generally getting to know more potters than you would normally see in a year. Finally there was cello music from Denis Moore accompanied by David Canter's wife Kay (who must have been exhausted after organising all those meals) and folk songs from Chris Charman of Godshill Pottery. Sheila and Mick Casson were there and his report ends 'May the CPA have many more such days ahead!' which indeed we had. They were almost all organised by David Canter.

▷ Letter from Bernard Leach to Rosemary Wren accepting an invitation to the CPA Winter Party held at the Arts Council Gallery during the Bernard Leach 50 year retrospective exhibition

▽ Cover and back of Newsletter 7, showing members and friends building 3 Lowndes Court, London, in 1959

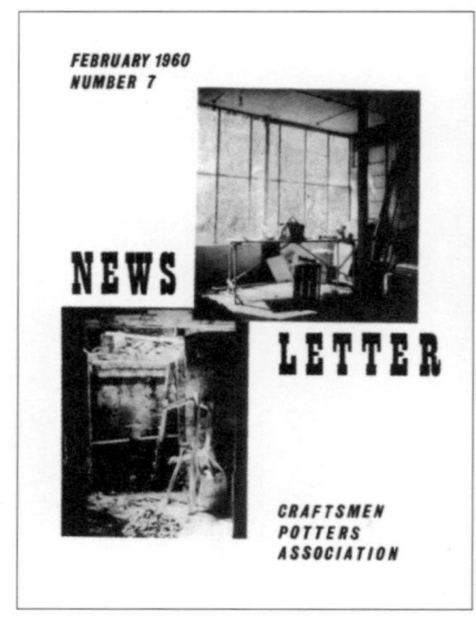

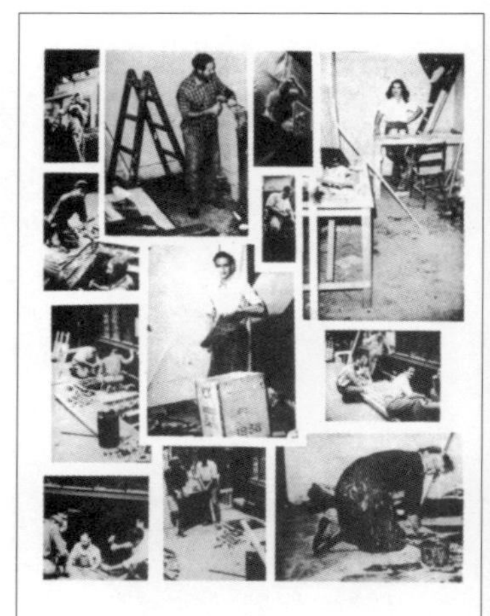

Later came the monthly evening meetings. The list speaks for itself of the generosity of time and thought put into them by so many speakers, all of whom gave freely of their time and expertise. Some took the form of an annual party at a London exhibition or museum. From 1960-4 they were my responsibility, then Murray Fieldhouse took over.

Mick Casson's sister Pan Henry was at that first Potters Day too. We were amazed and delighted to hear that she was prepared to manage our hypothetical shop. Also my mother brought forth an idea with a different emphasis for financing a shop: each potter contributing £5 to a premises fund would be entitled to take over a specially designed exhibition corner for a week. Their personal invitations would build up publicity, their demonstrations could add unique interest and they would learn about the shop. Everyone was in favour; eventually forty-eight people booked exhibitions and a total of seventy-four people contributed.

The CPA's first official AGM was on 4 April 1959. As Chairman I was able to announce that premises had been found. The first Craftsmen Potters Shop was at 3 Lowndes Court, Carnaby Street, in central London. About twenty people worked on its transformation during the year following for a total of 950 hours and more, but the brunt of the work was done by Mick Casson, Pan Henry (who did all the painting), Lawrence Keen, Anita Hoy, Eileen Lewenstein, Aubrey Coote and of course David Canter who designed and co-ordinated. Eventually, with elegant windows and general display, a carefully thought-out solo exhibition space and office on the ground floor, a members' room and compartments for work of their own choice downstairs, there it all was just as we had dreamed.

On 28 May 1960, two hundred people crowded in. Walter Lipton, justly proud, introduced Lady Glenconner, who made a brilliant opening speech surrounded by a distinguished Special Exhibition from Ray Finch of Winchcombe Pottery. A financial success from the day of opening, with an astonishing average of £80 a week retail sales reported by December, it remained our home with Pan Henry as manager for seven years.

By 1967 all available space was overflowing with pots and association office work: sales averaged £327 a week. We had to admit that our first shop was outgrown and look towards the possibility of even greater development in new and larger premises more prominently situated.

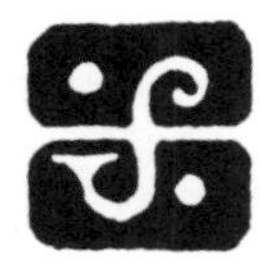

THE LEACH POTTERY

BERNARD LEACH
JANET LEACH

St. Ives, Cornwall.
Phone St. Ives 398

27. XII. 60

Dear Rosemary,

I hasten to let you know that I shall stay in London over Friday Jan. 13th & will therefore be able to come to your gathering that evening. I am afraid Janet, my wife, will have had to return to St. Ives.

A happy N. Year to you & your Mother. We go up for preparations tomorrow & this is written in haste

Yours

Bernard Leach

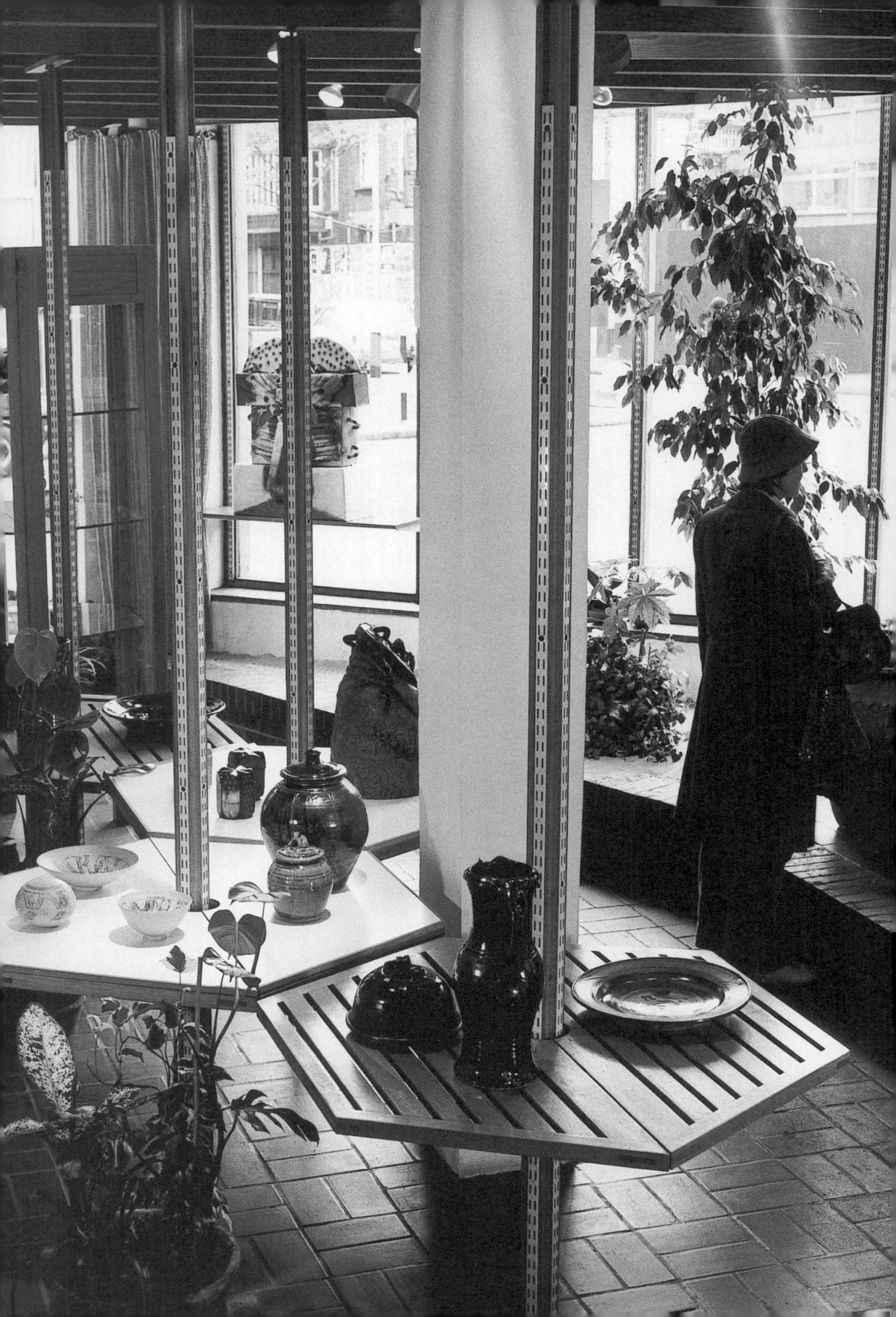

ON THE MOVE

by Michael Casson

"The next phase, say from the mid-seventies onwards, showed the association reflecting more and more the changes taking place in ceramics throughout the world"

The first ten years of the Craftsmen Potters Association was a time of great achievement. Through the enthusiasm of its members led by David Canter as honorary secretary, and backed by the organisational and selling skills of Pan Henry, the shop manager, the ideal of a co-operative for potters, run as far as possible by potters, was brought into existence. In 1967 the CPA moved location and embarked on a new period of expansion. The last few years of the sixties was a time of consolidation on which a sound reputation was built. But the next phase, say from the mid-seventies onwards, showed the association reflecting more and more the changes taking place in ceramics throughout the world and emerging in the eighties as the representative organisation for a wide spectrum of potters.

◁ The Craftsmen Potters Shop, William Blake House, Marshall Street, London, 1970

WILLIAM BLAKE HOUSE

In December 1967 the CPA took over its present premises in William Blake House on the corner of Broadwick and Marshall Streets, just a stone's throw from Carnaby Street. David Attenborough opened the new shop to a packed house of enthusiastic potters and public. The negotiations with Westminster Council carried out by the indefatigable David Canter were long and complicated and at their conclusion the hoped-for gallery area that was to have complemented the shop had to be abandoned because of the expense entailed. As with the first shop David designed the interior layout in a style appropriate to the times, English oak and warm clay tiles predominating.

If the building of the first shop was largely in the hands of three people, David Canter, Lawrence Keen and myself, ably helped by volunteers, it is true to say that this spirit still prevailed in 1967. Many potter members, and in particular Harrow students, helped David Canter (still in the thick of it all) even though professional builders were called upon for much of the work. It should be recorded that those who worked in the shop found it a delight; it showed off the pots, particularly the stonewares of the late sixties and early seventies to great advantage.

As the organisation flourished, the list of CPA events and exhibitions conveys only a flavour of the times. Robert Fournier, CPA archivist, has been an excellent source of reference. Attempting to record impressions of the association through these years means I can only mention a few of the people and happenings which produced, in all, a remarkable period of growth and expansion.

Over the whole of the fifty years there have been many Council members elected by their peers to take the chair at meetings held four times a year. Their duties did not end with Council meetings but involved working out more detailed policies as well as general planning. Looking at this list of names, and recalling just a few of the other Council members, it is evident that throughout its existence the Council has represented a healthy cross-section of potters working with clay in very different ways. Council members not only reflected as far as possible geographical representation (great efforts were made earlier to fulfil this ideal) but the various areas of ceramics: handbuilding, throwing, repetition, education and, moreover, robust to meticulous, functional to sculptural uses of clay.

A 1967 Council list featured 'Beano' Katharine Pleydell-Bouverie, Brigitta Appleby, Harry Horlock Stringer, Colin Pearson, Murray Fieldhouse, Alan Wallwork, Eileen Lewenstein, David Leach, Anita Hoy, Bryan Newman, John Reeve and Rosemary Wren with myself as Chair – a pretty varied group to work with. Later potters like Peter Dick, Colin Kellam, Mary Rogers and David Winkley were there. After David Canter's tragic death, David Winkley took over as Treasurer and used his expertise at a time of considerable crisis.

▷▽ The Craftsmen Potters Shop, 1970s

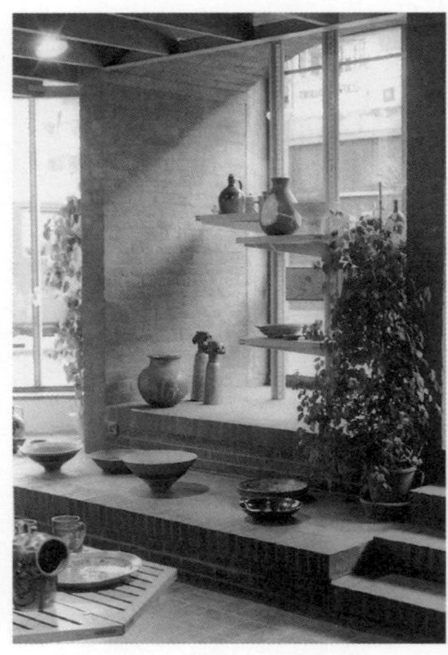

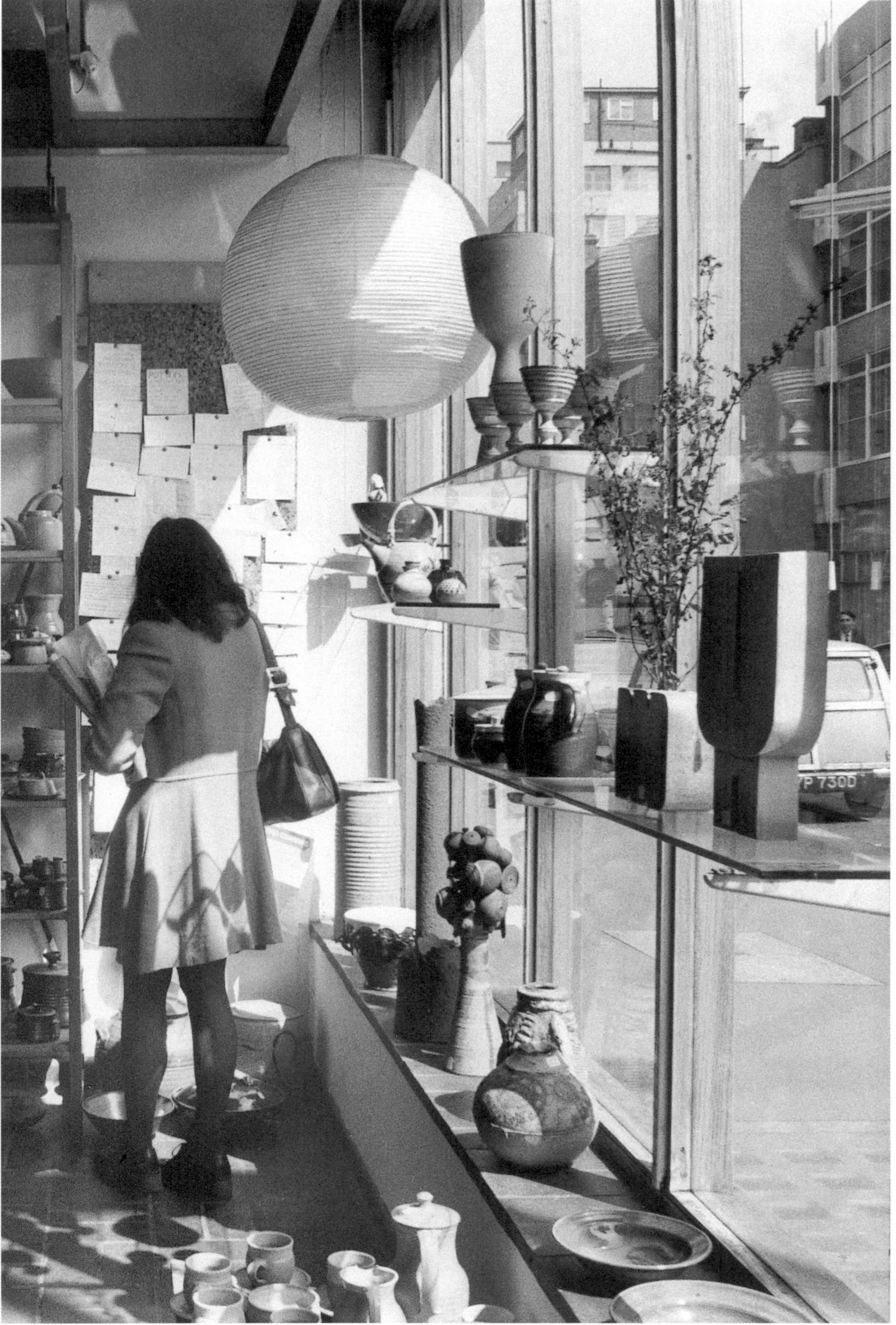
7P 730D

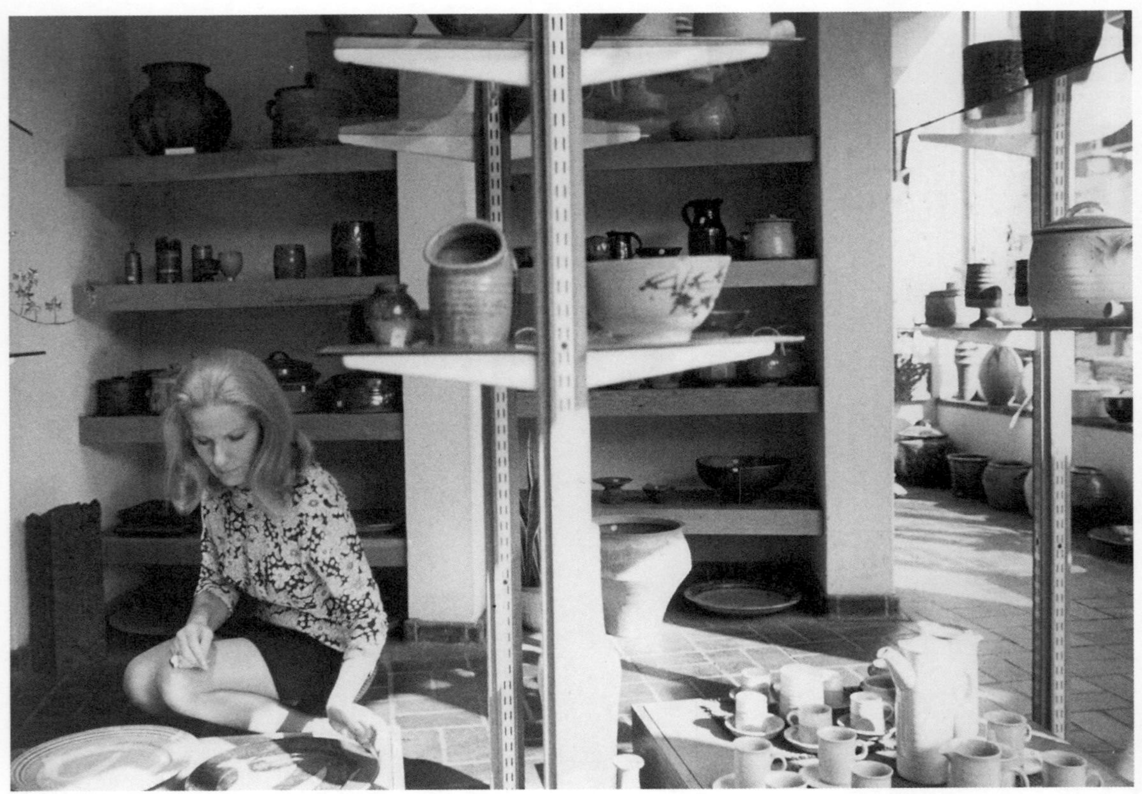

The CPA was indeed lucky to have such a cool head to call upon from its ranks of potters. The diversity and variety of Council members can be seen by looking at the lists of potters who put their ideas and energies at the service of the CPA in response to the membership who voted them onto the Council. You could see the organisation grow and broaden under their influence.

There have been several managers or directors of the shop. Pan Henry continued in Marshall Street until 1972 when Chris Palmer took over for three years until Stephen Brayne came in 1975. Later Marta Donaghey took over. Each has been concerned with the day to day running of the shop and the affairs of the association; they have all been lucky to have had dedicated staff. Pan Henry had the additional task before the days of *Ceramic Review* of getting together a regular Newsletter. In theory this was prepared by various Council members but more often than not it was a last-minute compilation of contributions by various members and friends which was put together by Pan Henry and her loyal staff. When, in 1969, Emmanuel Cooper and Eileen Lewenstein proposed that the time had come for a more professional magazine that they offered to edit, it gave the association a new and important publishing function. The first issue appeared in January 1970. *Ceramic Review* confirmed the outward-looking qualities of the association and responded to the ever widening interest in studio pottery.

◁ Pan Henry, shop manager, 1970

▽ The cover of the first issue of *Ceramic Review*, published in January 1970

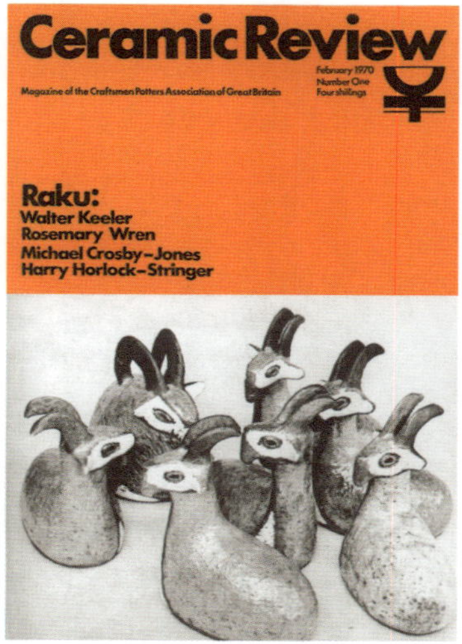

"The late 60s was the hey-day of the repetition domestic pot...customers regularly bought sets of pots, purchased goblets by the hundreds and mugs by the thousands"

Potters also began to respond to changes in the market, adapting to different tastes and styles. The late 60s was the heyday of the repetition domestic pot, often handsomely covered with creamy white dolomite and black iron temmoku glaze. Customers regularly bought sets of pots, purchased goblets by the hundreds and mugs by the thousands. Ceramic sculpture, for even then no one really knew what to call it, was on display and found a small but devoted market with Gordon Baldwin, Bryan Newman and Alan Wallwork continually coming up with new ideas and forms. By the early seventies potters who had trained at pottery courses such as those at Harrow School of Art were able to earn a living from making domestic pots. Often they relied on sales from the CPA shop for a considerable part of their incomes.

REPUTATION

By the eighties the shop had gained a reputation which brought managers and directors of shops and galleries from all over the world to make selections of work; export orders were negotiated as far afield as Australia, USA and Japan. All of this continues today, but ten years ago gradually, and then with gathering momentum, it marked further changes in the association. The range of work has widened, colours have changed and new styles have appeared. Side by side with repetition domestic stoneware, toasted unglazed surfaces or celadon glazes, there are more decorative earthenwares and colourful stonewares plus many one-off pieces, vessels as well as sculptural forms; above all perhaps it is the advent of porcelain that has given a different look to the shelves and general display at the CPA in the eighties, and for that we have to thank David Leach more than anyone else; his throwable medium-temperature porcelain body was made commercially available and was followed by others.

COMMUNICATION

Activities taken on by the CPA have helped to put pots and potters before a wider public. Communication has been the keynote, achieved through exhibitions, evening meetings, fairs, workshops and many other sorts of events. Potters, full-time and part-time, professional, experienced, students and amateurs, have contributed to and become aware and informed of the latest ceramic ideas. Exhibitions have ranged from the major one person shows to group exhibitions, window

▷ Walter Keeler building a raku kiln at a Potters Camp, c1975

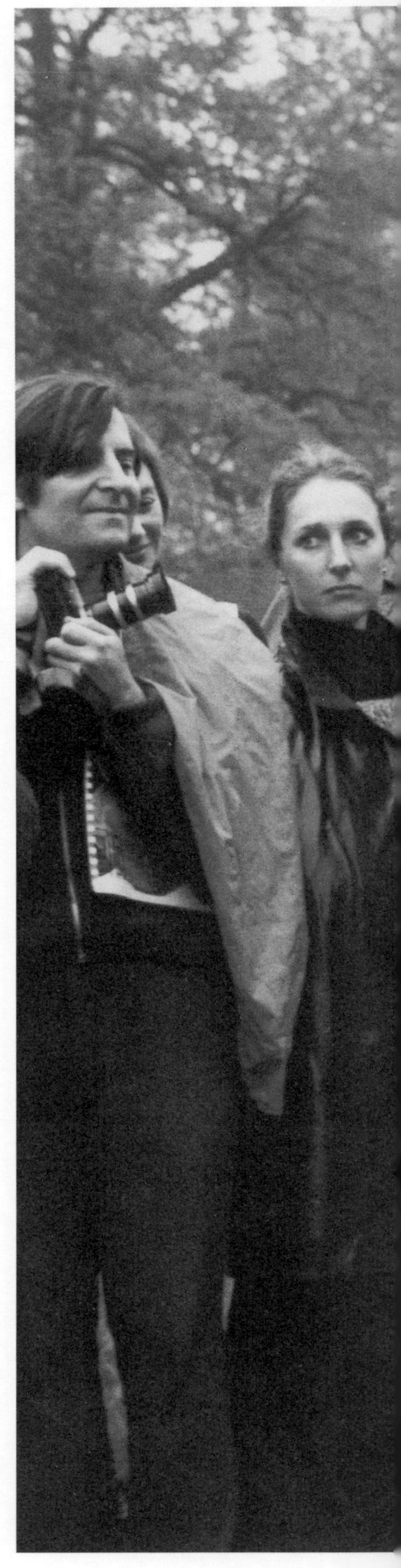

displays and 'theme' shows like cooking pots, teapots, candlesticks or boxes. Exhibitions have been arranged to coincide with the publication of new books by full members; and have included Alan Caiger-Smith's wonderful *Tin Glaze Pottery in Europe and the Islamic World* (Faber and Faber, 1973).

Peter Lane's ground-breaking book *Studio Ceramics* launched an exhibition of work by over fifty potters. Groups of potters outside the CPA have been invited to exhibit: the South Wales Potters, itself brought into existence by help from the CPA and its South Wales member Frank Hamer; or groups of potters from Canada, France and Germany. At one point, the New Members show was a regular feature, demonstrating the growth of the association and its seeking out and acceptance of new ideas. The CPA took on the daunting task of helping to arrange the *International Exhibition of Ceramics* at the Victoria and Albert Museum in 1972. My memory has not faded yet of one of the judges, Hans Coper, leaning back, perhaps swooning might be a better word, at the sight of hundreds and hundreds of pots and 'objects' unpacked and sitting on top of their wrappings waiting for us to 'judge' them.

Evening meetings, wide ranging in subject matter and usually by experts, were often held, appropriately, at the Art Workers Guild in Queen Square. Recalling just a few gives the flavour of these events, which have helped to give information, spread understanding about pottery and generally delight a growing number of people – not only potters by any means. Michael Cardew's three talks on Pottery in West Africa were memorable, as was Daniel Rhodes lecture on the avant-garde pots of the United States. Emmanuel Cooper, Robert Fournier and Derek Royle headed a 'brains trust' on technical matters, to be

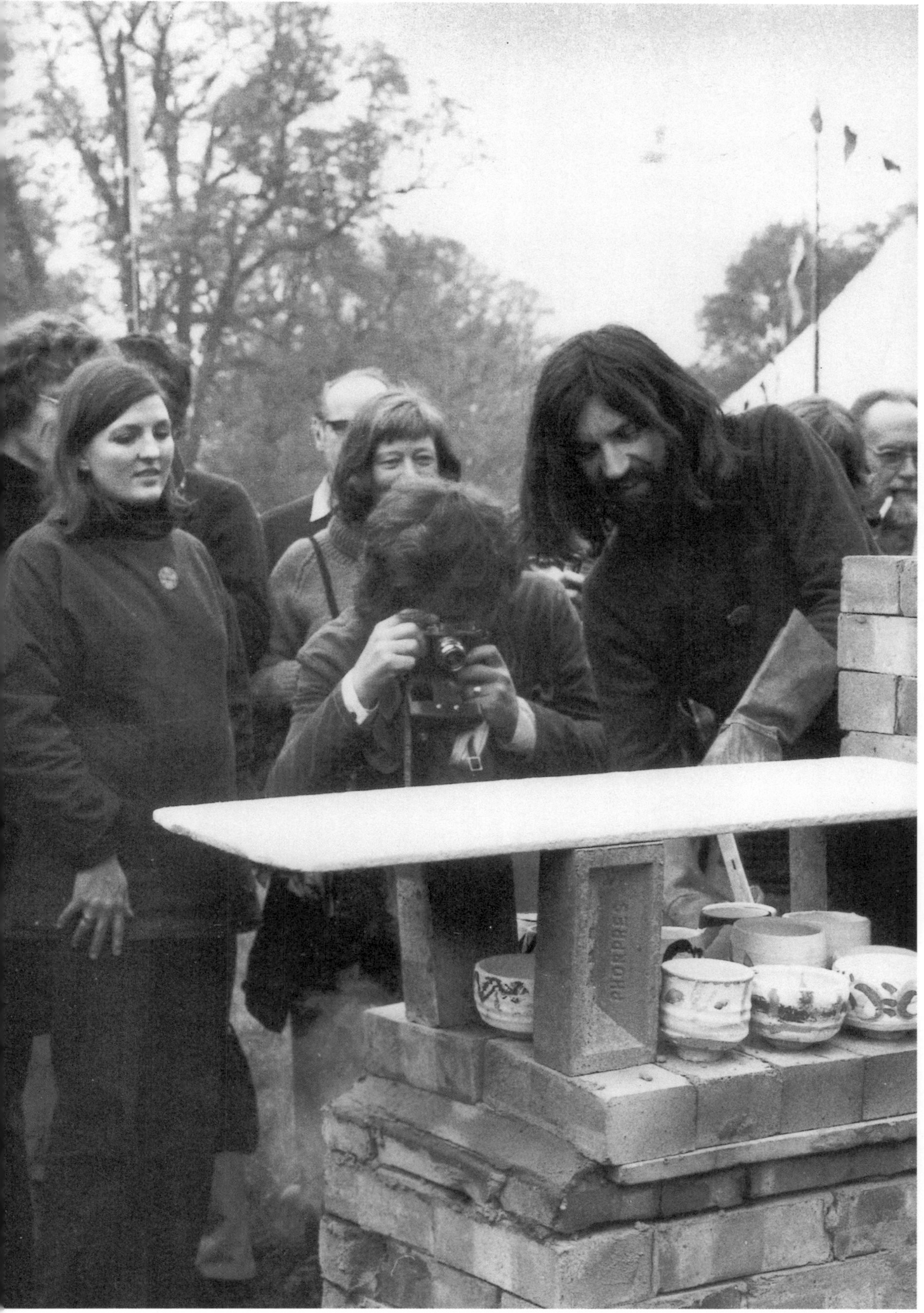
PHORPRES

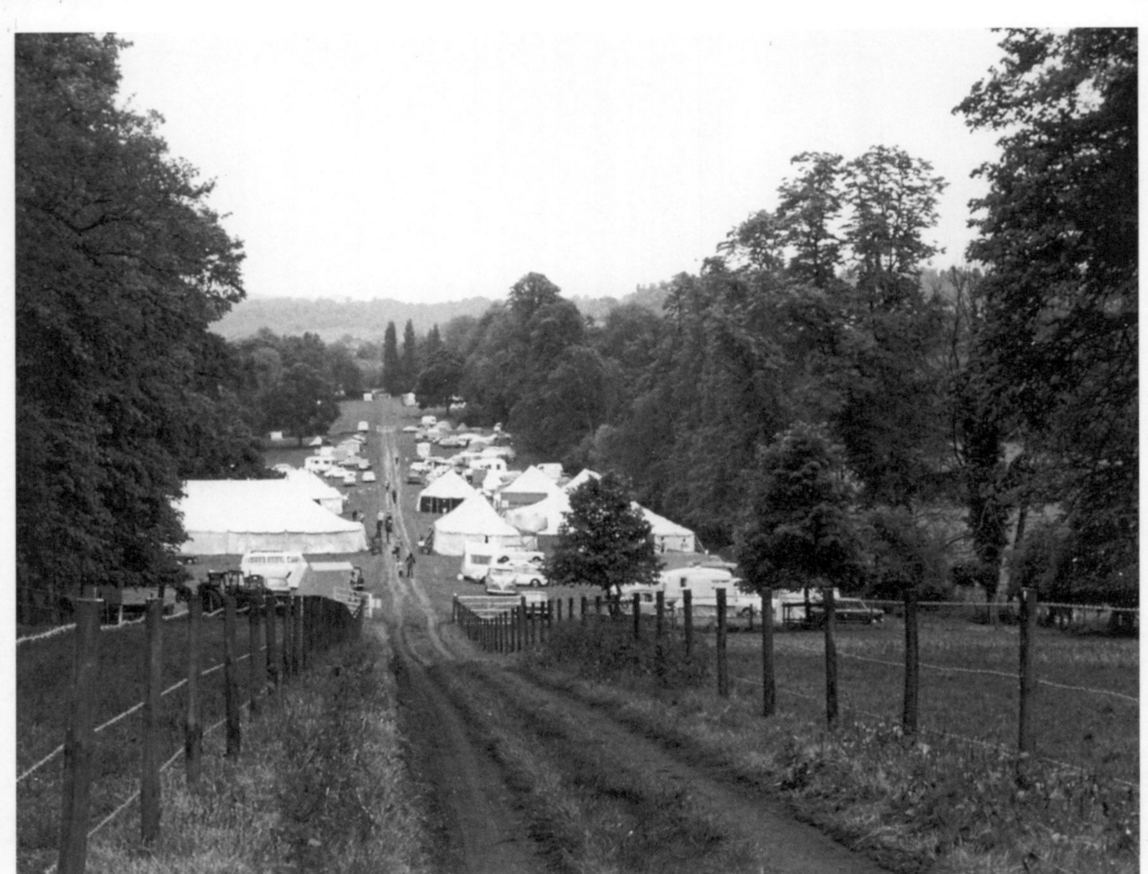

followed with one on Workshop Practice with Harry Horlock Stringer, David Eeles, Barbara Cass and Peter Dick. Bob Rogers stimulated much thought when he spoke about Freedom and Design in Craft, whilst Tony Hepburn showed Modern American Ceramics, followed later by Bill Ismay on A Collector's Point of View. Virtually all aspects of how to use clay, glaze, fire – and why – have been covered.

Other events too, have helped to bring potters closer together whilst letting a wider and wider circle of people know about pottery. When Bernard Leach finally agreed to join the CPA as an honorary member he said he was joining us because we had 'good fellowship' – an important part of the make-up of the association. Events such as the 1968 Potters Day hosted by Harry Horlock Stringer at Taggs Yard in Barnes were highly significant. Potters Days led on to David Canter's idea of the Potters Camps: three were held at Loseley Park, Surrey, two at Dartington, Devon, (including the mammoth multi-craft – wood, glass, calligraphy, textiles) – from 1973 to 1982. These occasions have proved immeasurably popular and have helped foster the caring CPA image. Meetings for full members and associates at Dillington House in Somerset, Dartington in Devon and above all at West Dean in West Sussex have proved that potters can relate to each other across a spectrum that ranges now from functional domestic and garden ware to

"Denise Wren had listed several categories under which a pot could be judged and each category had many questions or points that could be asked about the work. I remember a figure of eighty-seven points"

◁ Potters Camp at Losely Park, c1970

▽ Potters Camp at Dartington, 1976. Left to right: Sheila Casson, David Canter, David Winkley

innovative one-off ceramics. Long may this communication continue. Film festivals, demonstrations of potting techniques in the shop, and more, extend the list of activities showing a similar commitment.

SILVER JUBILEE

Studio Ceramics Today, the exhibition at the Victoria and Albert Museum in 1983 commemorating the CPA's silver jubilee, made the point again that all the efforts over the years helped establish new standards of excellence, both technical and aesthetic. This aim has always been a major concern of the CPA and one story illustrates the at times anguished struggles members have faced in improving the quality of work (sometimes selection processes literally took all day and all night). I have a memory of a meeting the Council called to try and find a definitive way of judging work.

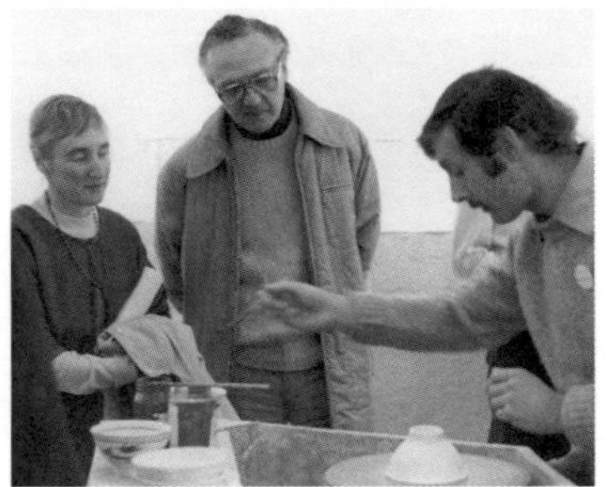

We invited Denise Wren and Bernard Leach, the doyens of their day, to come along and tell us how they thought work should be judged. Denise Wren, in an amazing piece of critical analysis, had listed several categories under which a pot could be judged and each category had many questions or points that could be asked about the work. I remember a figure of eight-seven points; it was a brilliant piece of planning. Bernard Leach thought a judge should ask one question 'has the pot heart?' The meeting ended, eventually, and the CPA has tried ever since to enquire what is a good pot, without finding an easy answer. So the question remains – what is a good piece of work?

CHANGE

While this heart searching and questioning was proceeding inside the CPA the world of ceramics outside was also changing. The CPA did not ignore these developments. Membership over the years has reflected differences in education, in market demands and reactions to outside influences such as the first sightings of ceramics from the USA in 1960.

In the world of education, which I believe to be a major influence in shaping ceramics, there have been crucial developments. In the late 1960s the Diploma in Art and Design (Dip AD) was giving way to more scholarly based BA (Hons) courses. Vocational training courses such as the one which sprang up at Harrow School of Art as well as in other schools responded to a need. In the event, innovative ceramics and domestic pottery were both well served. Hans Coper was teaching at

▷ Poster advertising *Studio Ceramics Today* at the Victoria and Albert Museum, 1983

▽ Vivienne Whitaker and Sue Taylor in the CPA shop, 1983

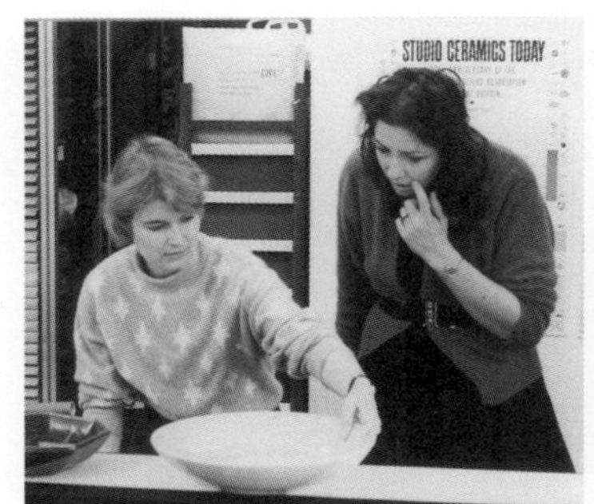

the Royal College of Art and a small but significant group of potters was about to emerge from there in the early seventies. Since then the number of BA (Hons) centres continued to grow and the cumulative effect of this and a number of other new factors has had far-reaching results today.

In 1971 Lord Eccles set up the Crafts Advisory Committee, later to become the Crafts Council, which was headed by potter Victor Margrie, with the brief to promote the artist-craftsman and stimulate growing public awareness of crafts. The Crafts Council has always helped both traditional and innovative craftspeople, especially the young – this is their investment in the future of crafts. By the mid 70s *Crafts* magazine alongside *Ceramic Review* and a growing body of literature about ceramics was showing an increasing number of new ceramics as well as traditional forms. Galleries selling individual pieces rather than repetition domestic ware were starting up all over the country. At the Victoria and Albert Museum the Crafts Council opened a Craft Shop and other centres followed. Sotheby's and other auction houses started to take an interest in crafts as Fine Art. The market had changed.

Sometimes economic recession seemed to underline new forces at work in the pottery community. All these factors, though lying beyond the control of the CPA or indeed anyone, have nevertheless been reflected in the association itself; by the influx of new kinds of potters to its ranks, the changing display facilities and a completely new refurbishment. It would need a Maynard Keynes of the ceramic world to evaluate how the confluence of these events, education, promotional, economic and aesthetic have affected and influenced each other. Which came first – the buyer or the pot? Through all these changes, the CPA has not only survived but grown in stature. It has to thank the hard work of its members, the support given by a host of associate members and friends and the guidance received from many loyal and hard-working individuals. Long may it flourish, and long may potters of all kinds meet and hold dialogue with each other.

This is an edited vesion of an essay written in 1983

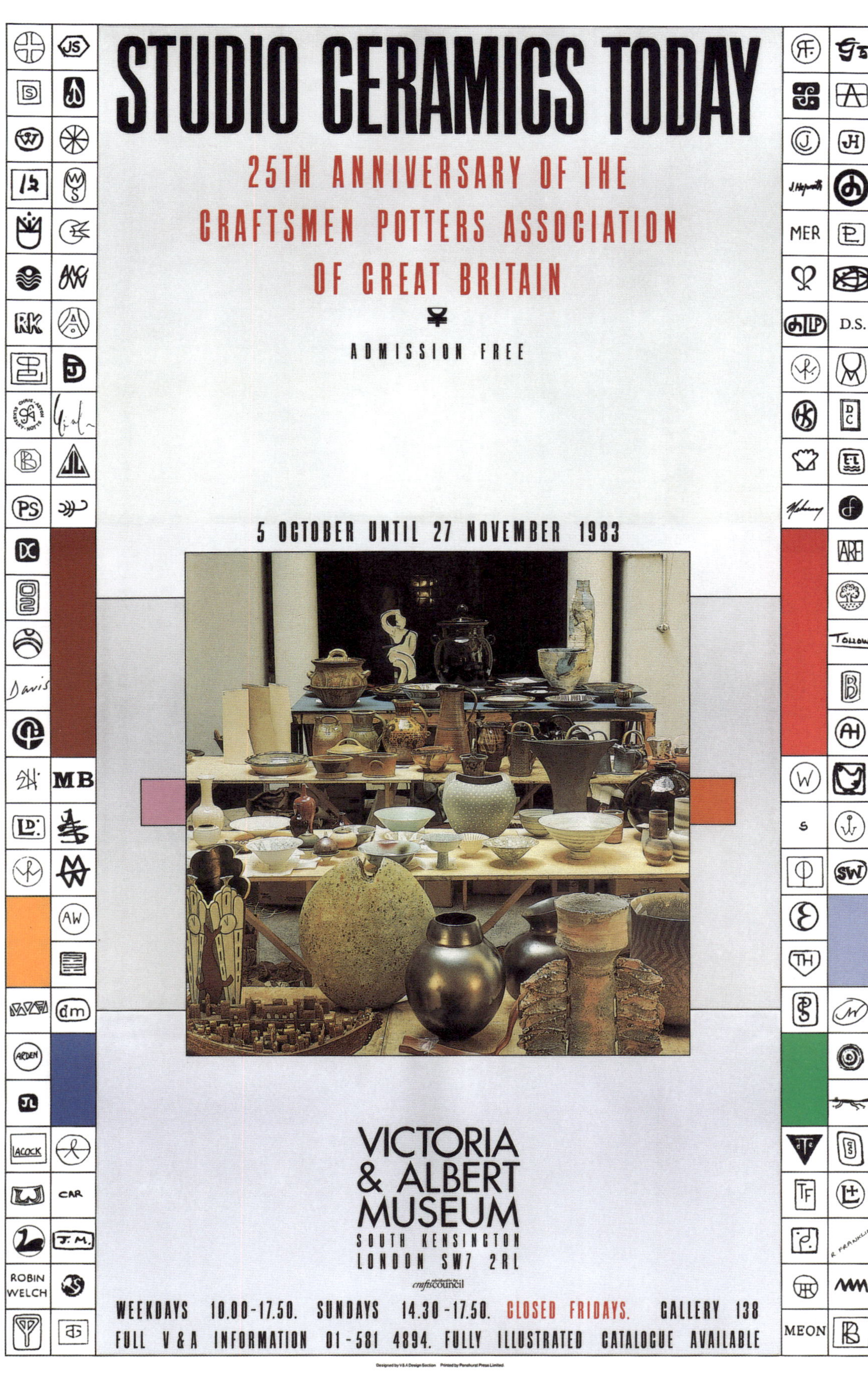
STUDIO CERAMICS TODAY
25TH ANNIVERSARY OF THE
CRAFTSMEN POTTERS ASSOCIATION
OF GREAT BRITAIN
ADMISSION FREE
5 OCTOBER UNTIL 27 NOVEMBER 1983
VICTORIA
& ALBERT
MUSEUM
SOUTH KENSINGTON
LONDON SW7 2RL
craftscouncil
WEEKDAYS 10.00-17.50. SUNDAYS 14.30-17.50. CLOSED FRIDAYS. GALLERY 138
FULL V&A INFORMATION 01-581 4894. FULLY ILLUSTRATED CATALOGUE AVAILABLE
Designed by V&A Design Section
Printed by Penshurst Press Limited.

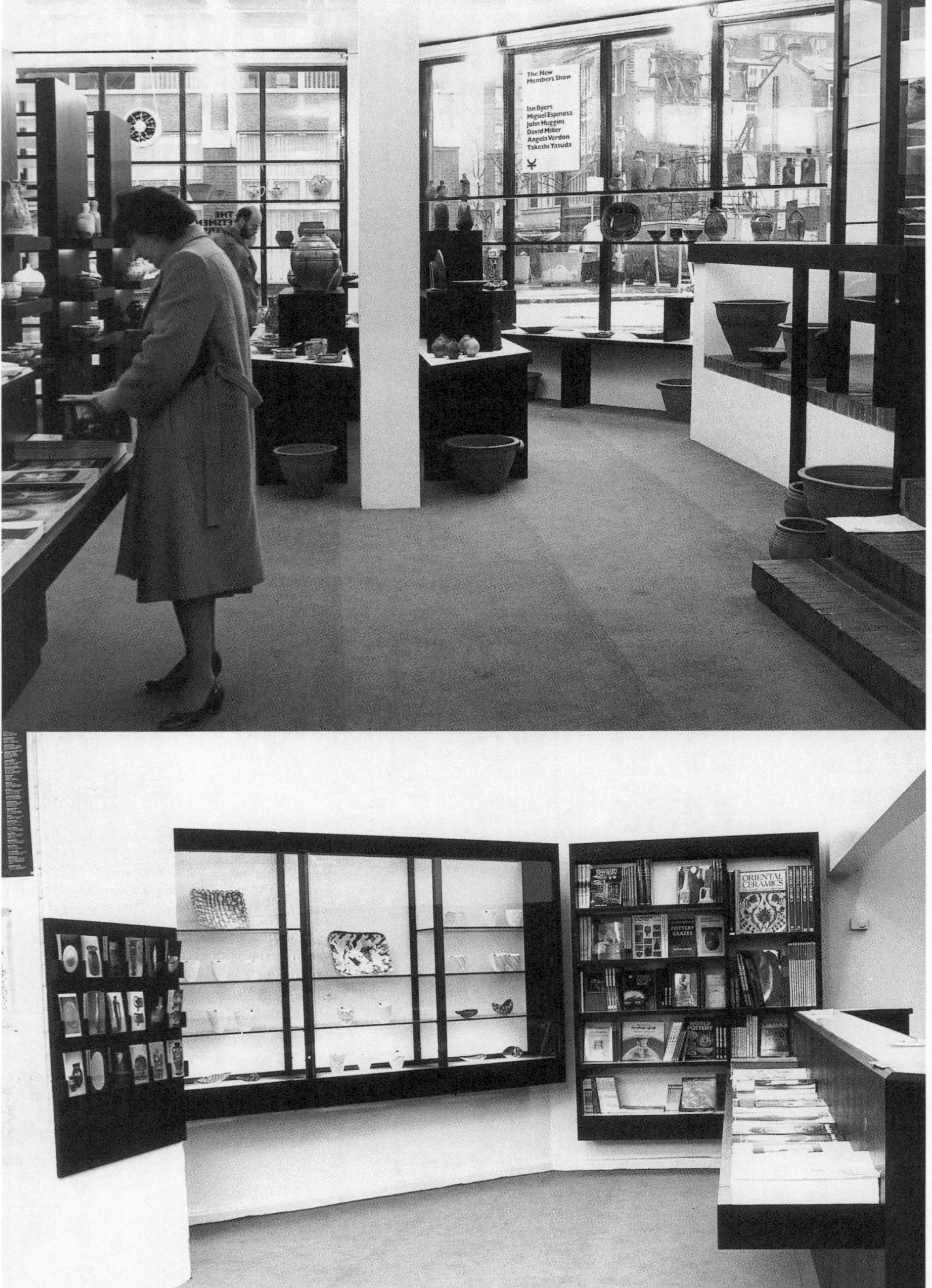
The New Members Show
Ian Byers
Miguel Espinosa
John Huggins
David Miller
Angela Verdon
Takeshi Yasuda
ORIENTAL CERAMICS
POTTERY GLAZES
WORLD POTTERY

PAST PRESENT FUTURE

by Jonathan Sidney

"The 1980s saw a period of consolidation for the Craft Potters Association, dealing with the past but aware that it was necessary to face the future"

◁ Ron Carter's design for the CPA shop, 1983

The 1980s saw a period of consolidation for the Craft Potters Association, dealing with the past but aware that it was necessary to face the future. Feeling that David Canter's classic design for the Craftsmen Potters Shop needed bringing more in tune with current thinking within the art/craft world, in 1983 the leading designer Ron Carter was commissioned to produce a new layout and image for the interior of the shop and gallery. The entire interior was redesigned and rebuilt in black elm, a wood that beautifully set off the colour and texture of the pots. The individual stock shelves for potters were retained, although in a different format. The false ceiling was removed to give a more airy space.

A diverse series of educational talks and demonstrations was arranged by the then events secretary Vanessa Wills. These included talks by Harry Davis, James Tower and Oliver Watson, who was then head of ceramics at the V&A. Special exhibitions at the shop included work by Takeshi Yasuda, Alan Caiger-Smith, Janice Tchalenko and John Ward. Each week a series of talks and or demonstrations – Potter in the Shop – added a further useful dimension to illuminating the work of potters. In the late 1980s the rear part of the shop was converted into the David Canter Gallery, named after the association's first honorary secretary. This useful

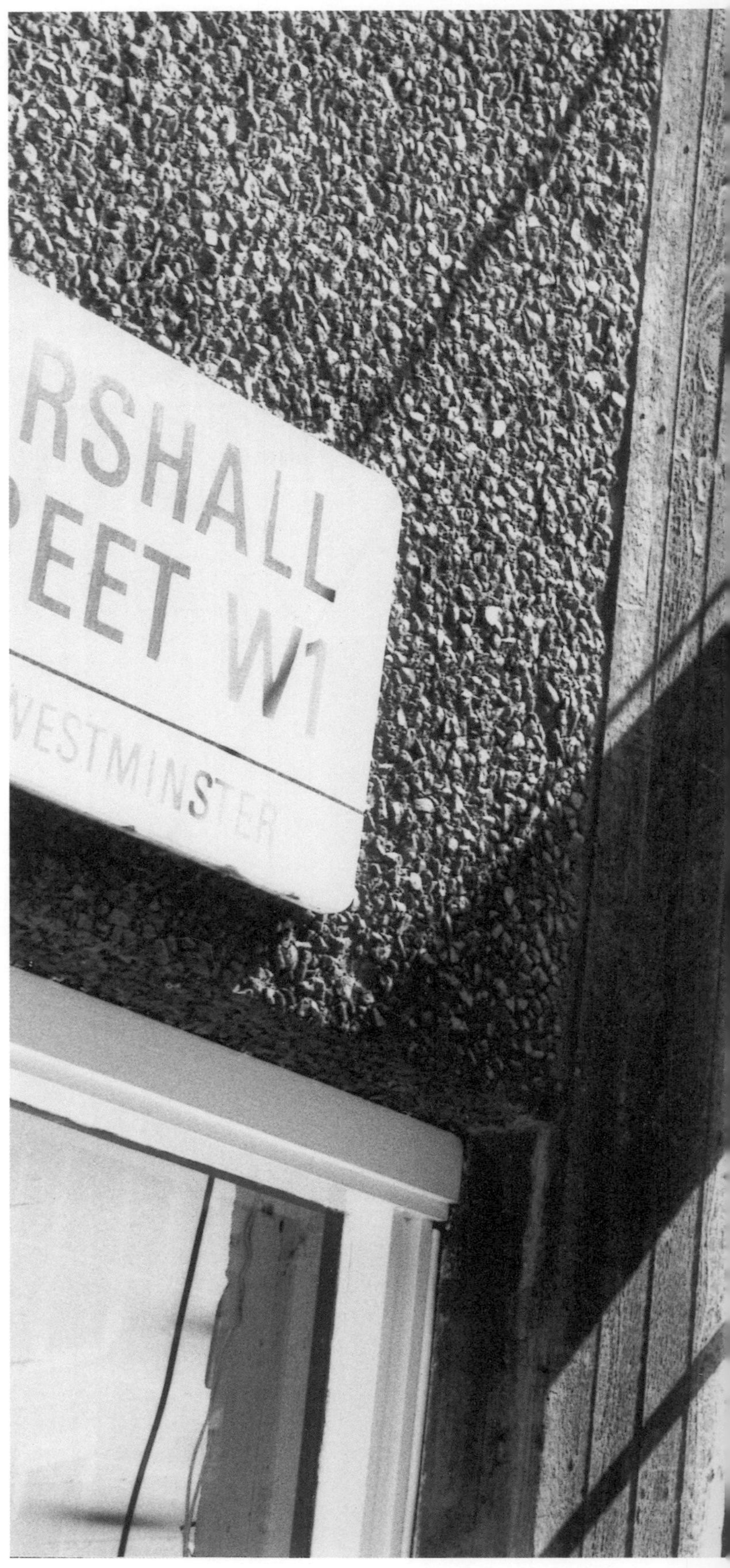

▷ Sign for the newly renamed Contemporary Ceramics with pot by Denise Wren, c1991

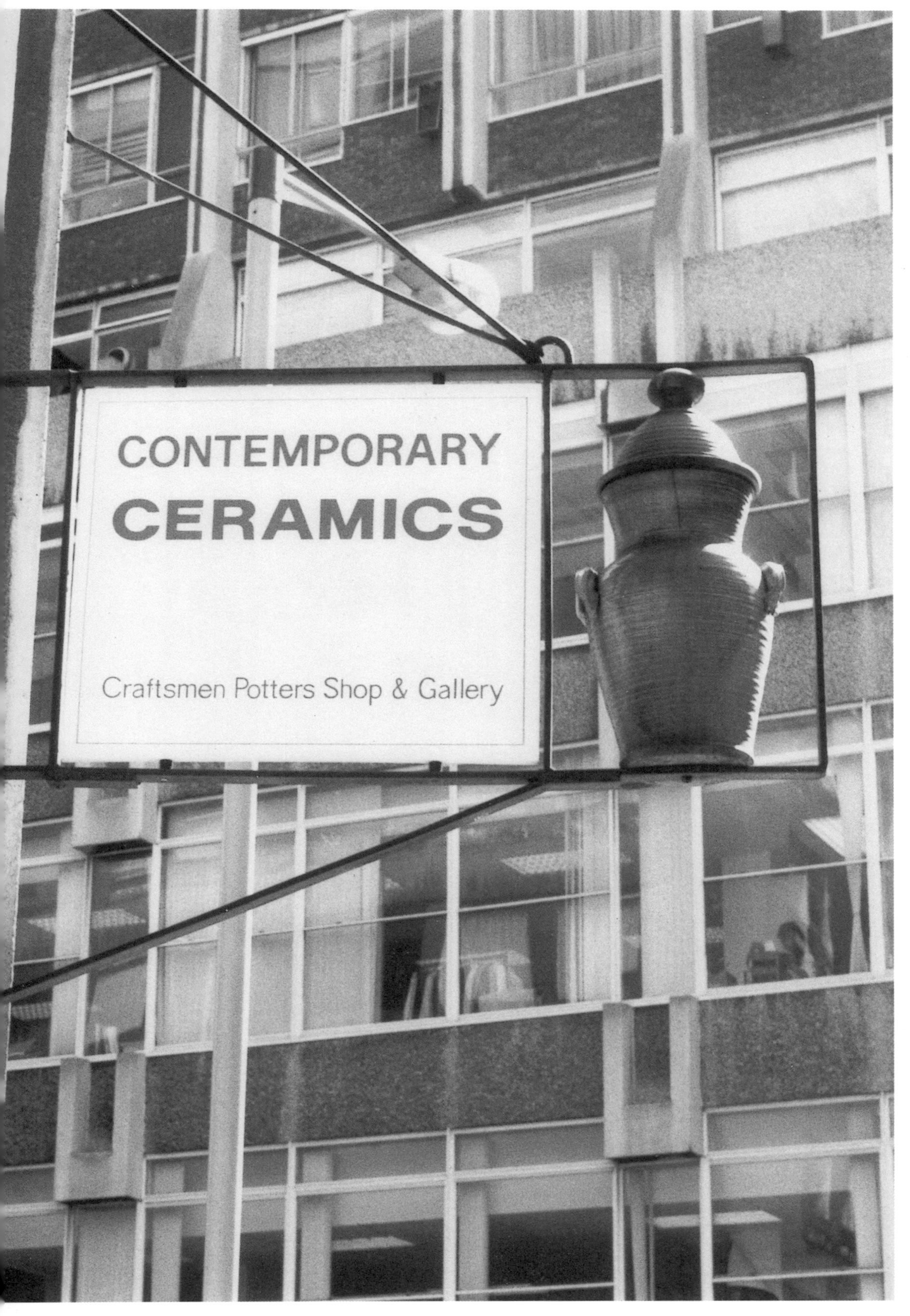
CONTEMPORARY
CERAMICS
Craftsmen Potters Shop & Gallery

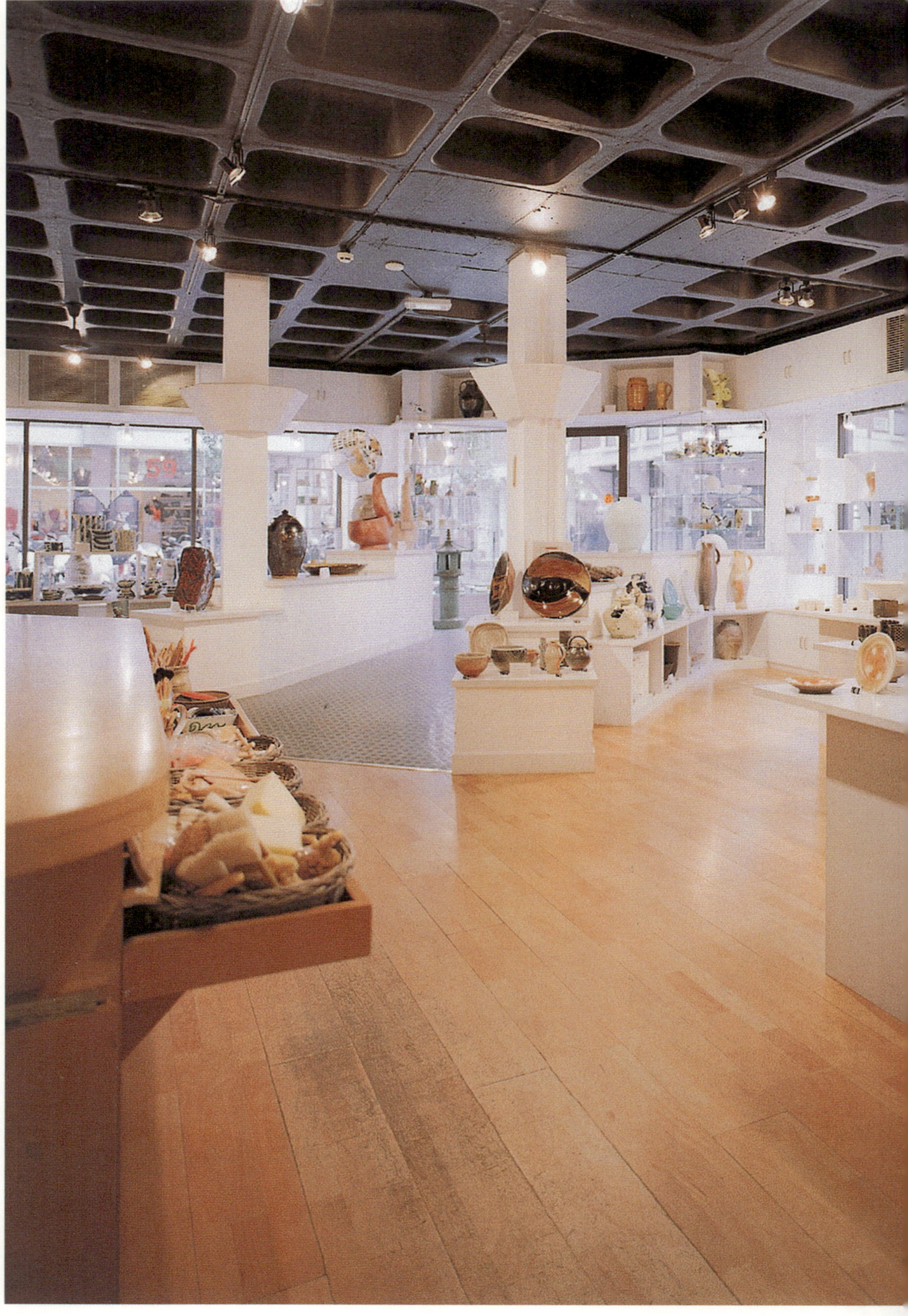
59

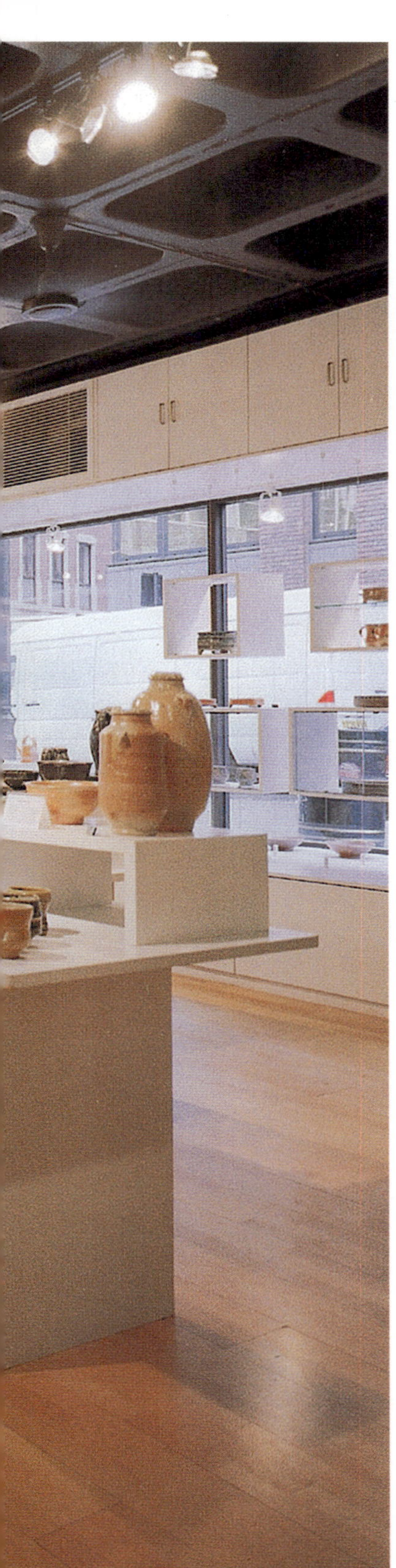

◁ The redesigned interior of Contemporary Ceramics, 1998

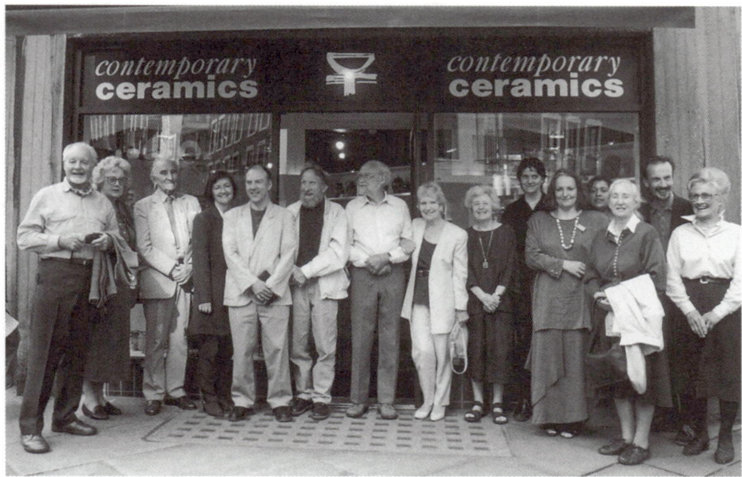

▽ The reopening of the shop, 1997. From left: Harry Horlock Stringer, Liz Gale, David Leach, Gaynor Linsey, Jack Doherty, Mick Casson, Ray Finch, Pan Casson, Eileen Lewenstein, Jo Bergman, Marta Donaghey, Claire Dixon, Sheila Casson, David Whiting, Ann Townsend

space more clearly identified a gallery setting for both individual and mixed exhibitions.

For one memorable weekend event, the American potter John Glick demonstrated his unique methods of working, the tools he used and his inventive use of slips, stamps and glazes. The occasion was remembered as much for the Brixton Riots that took place near the venue as the highly innovative and imaginative skills carried out so adroitly by John Glick. There was also a residential weekend at Keele University on Aspects of Marketing, and a visit to the fine collections held at the Fitzwilliam Museum and Kettles Yard in Cambridge.

THE 1990s

The CPA faced the nineties with over thirty years trading experience behind it, and with confidence in the future of the craft. A wide number of changes to the structure and organisation of the association were introduced by the Council. The first was a change of name for the association to Craft Potters Association. This was widely thought to be more appropriate in the age of equality and better reflected the mood and ethos of the CPA. In 1990 the shop also adopted a new name – Contemporary Ceramics: the Craft Potters Shop and Gallery. This more clearly reflected the way it operated, and more plainly defined what the shop did.

Further significant developments took place in 1997 with the award of £100,000 Lottery Grant to enable the Council to commission a

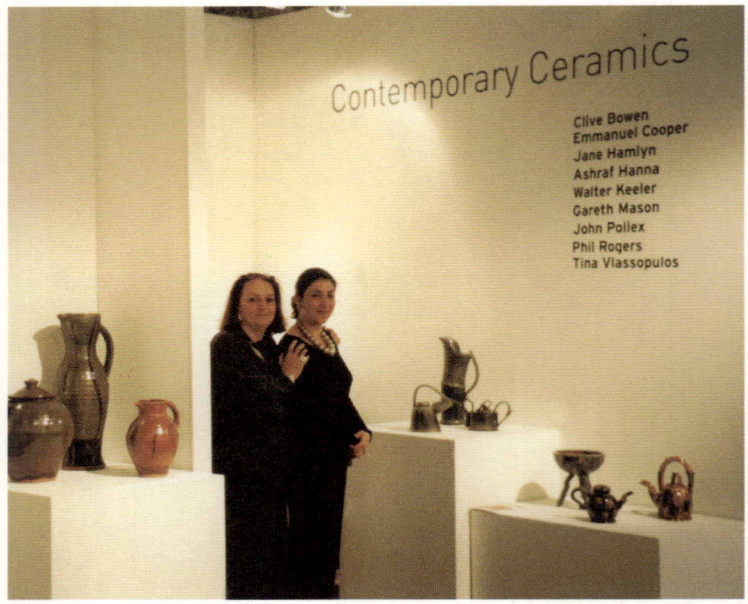

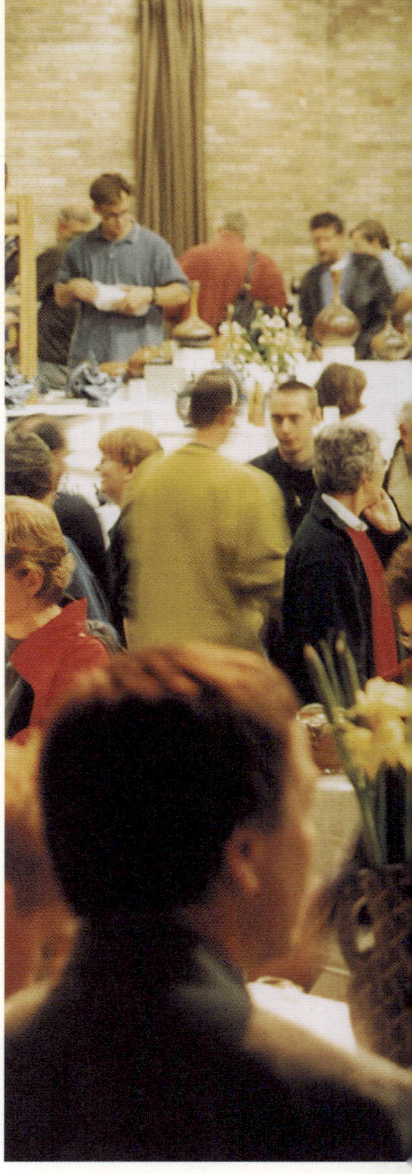

further redesign of the interior of Contemporary Ceramics. In addition to innovative ways of displaying work, the entrance was moved to the corner of Broadwick and Marshall Streets and a ramp was added, giving easy disabled access. The new arrangement, open, fresh and bright, showing some of the finest ceramics in the country, proved an instant success with the public.

Within the membership, new categories were introduced – that of full member, known as fellows, and that of members, known as professional members. Both categories had full voting rights, but this extended and opened up the number of potters who could take part in the organisation. Equally useful was the setting up of two trading companies, one dealing with the retail activities of Contemporary Ceramics, the other with the publishing activities of *Ceramic Review*. All continued under the watchful eye of the elected Council of the CPA, the potters who gave their time and energy to maintaining the democratic and fair basis on which the CPA was founded.

In the 1990s the CPA, in partnership with Rufford Ceramic Centre, Nottinghamshire, initiated the *Ceramic Fair*, aimed at introducing the general public to studio ceramics. In addition to the many stands by selected potters a lively and imaginative exhibition programme informed as well as entertained. Rufford Ceramic Centre subsequently took over running and organising the event. Later the CPA set up *Oxford Studio Ceramics* along similar lines, based at St Edward's School, Oxford, showing the work of some sixty selected makers. Again, a full education programme added to the attraction of the weekend. This highly successful event is now seen as a valuable and important part of the CPA's interaction with the public in seeking to promote the work of individual makers and to find new audiences.

△ *Oxford Studio Ceramics*, 1999

◁ Contemporary Ceramics stand at *Collect*, Victoria and Albert Museum, London, 2004

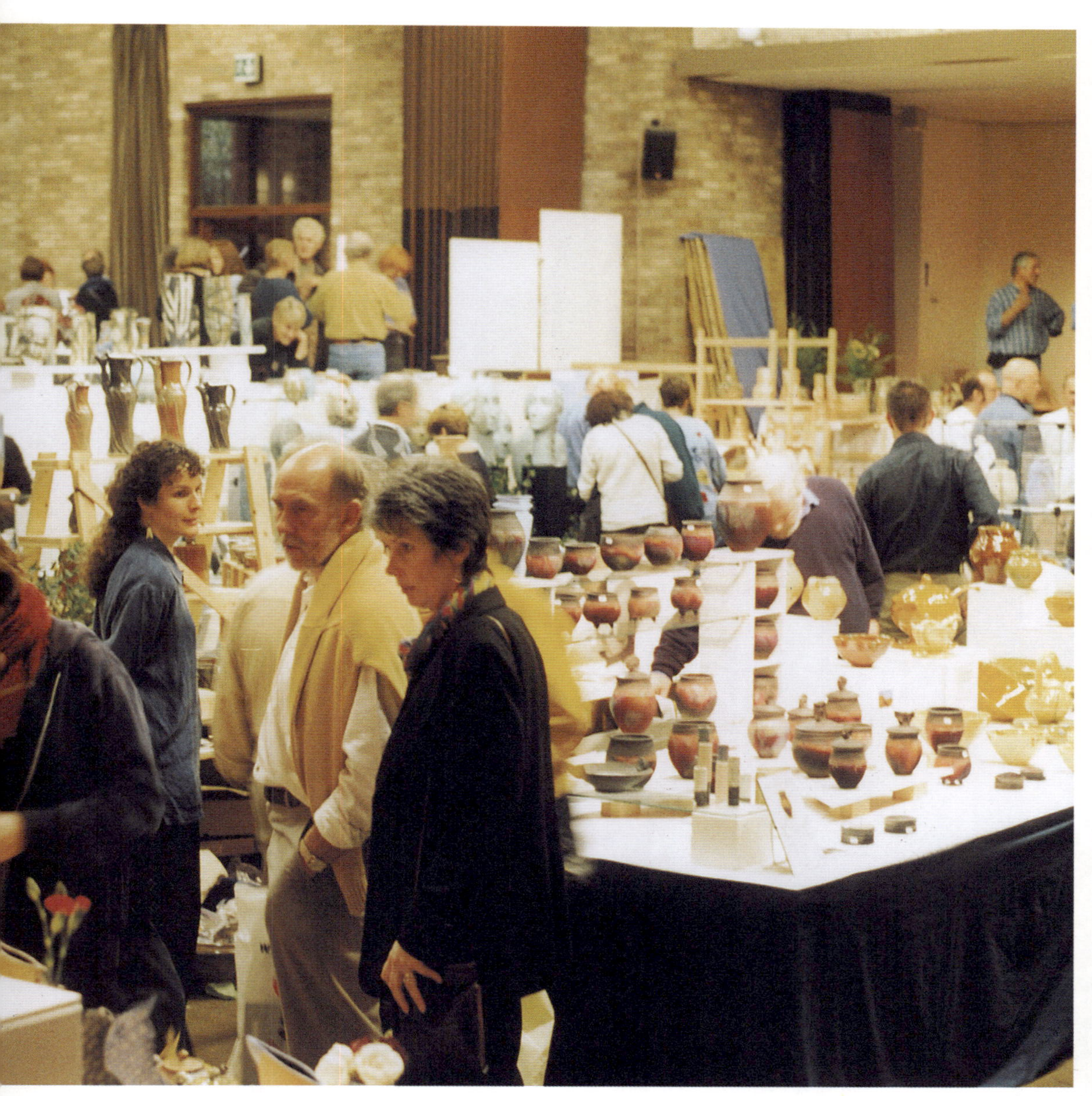

In 1991 the CPA set up the Craft Pottery Charitable Trust to support its educational activities. Trustees included a member of the Crafts Council and former officials and current members of the CPA. Funding for the Charitable Trust comes from donations from the CPA operating companies and from personal donations, bequests and other fund raising activities organised and supported by members. The Trust has several grant schemes, including an annual award of grants up to £1,000 in value, as well as occasional awards such as the Mick Casson Memorial Award for functional ware.

Each year, at Contemporary Ceramics, the CPA organises a Setting Out exhibition, which is designed to launch new graduates on their ceramics careers. Colleges are invited to submit the work of two

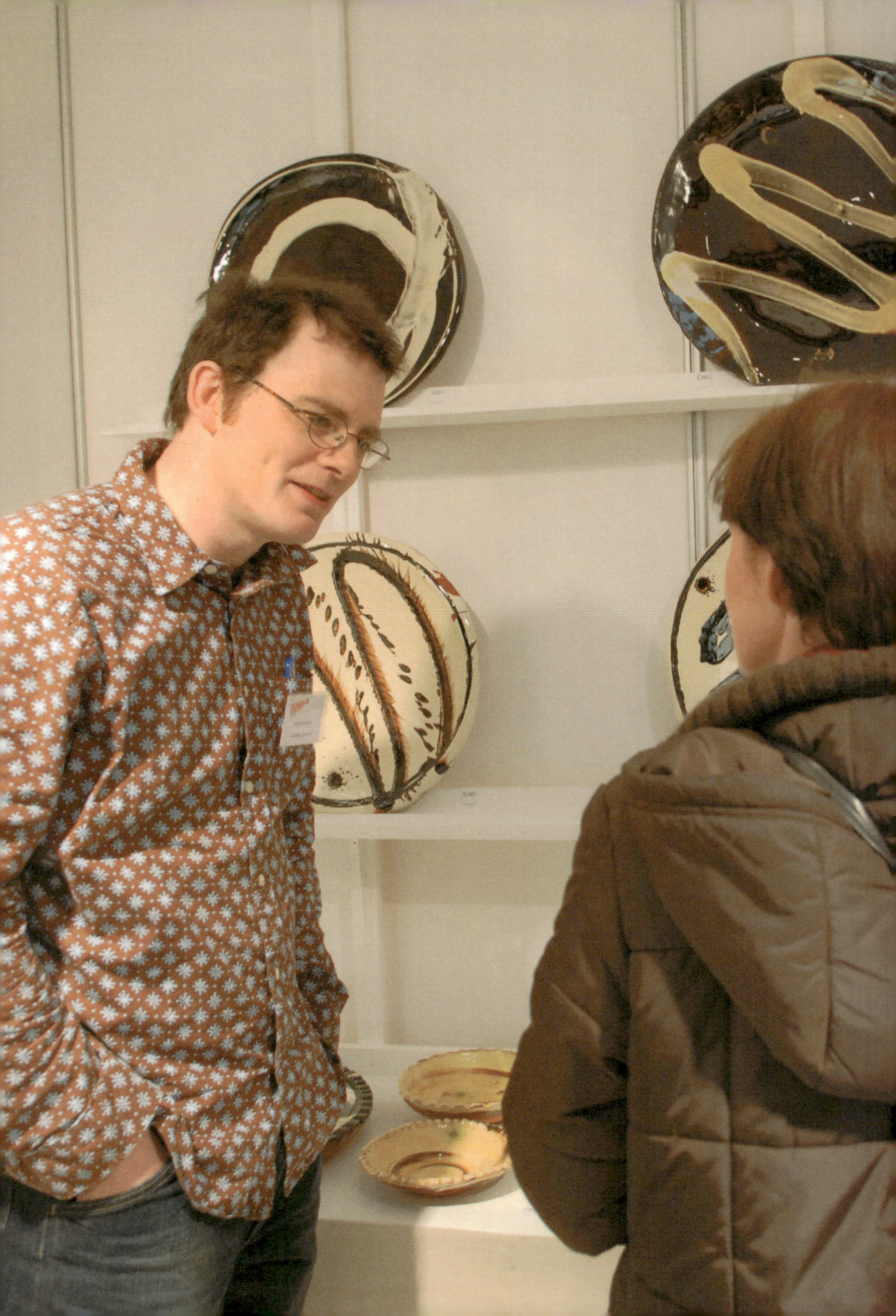

◁ Dylan Bowen with customer, *Ceramic Art London 2006*

students for selection for the exhibition. The entrants may also apply to the Charitable Trust for a bursary of up to £500 to enable them to carry out individual postgraduate projects.

Weekend events included a two-day festival of European ceramics, which reflected the international scope of the association. A special publication for members and friends was started with the publication of *CPA News*, which features information about CPA activities, news of new members, details of exhibitions and suchlike, plus articles by individual members.

"With a well-established sales outlet – Contemporary Ceramics – and publishing arm – Ceramic Review Publishing – the CPA was in a sound position to face the challenges of the new millennium"

THE NEW MILLENNIUM

With a well-established sales outlet – Contemporary Ceramics – and publishing arm – Ceramic Review Publishing – the CPA was in a sound position to face the challenges of the new millennium. *Ceramic Review* continued to publish a wide range of books in addition to the six issues of the magazine each year. These included twelve editions of *Potters: the Illustrated Directory of Fellows and Members of the Craft Potters Association*. In 2006, this publication adapted a new, small, compact format and a different name – *The Ceramics Book* – which was well-received, again introducing the work of CPA members to a wider audience. Other publications included *Potters' Tips*, *Clays and Glazes*, *A Guide to Public Collections of Studio Pottery in the British Isles*, *Lucie Rie* and, in 2006, *Janet Leach: A Potter's Life*.

In 2005 the association initiated *Ceramic Art London*, a major new international showcase for studio ceramics, at the Royal College of Art on 6-8 May 2005. Sir Christopher Frayling performed the opening ceremony, and he spoke about the value and importance of such events in finding new audiences and in promoting the work of some of the finest potters in the country. A highlight of the educational programme was a lecture followed by a question and answer session with Turner prize winning artist Grayson Perry, presentations that required an overspill hall to accommodate public interest.

Fairs in 2006 and 2007 built on this success, establishing *Ceramic Art London* as an important event that has made a valuable contribution to the understanding and enjoyment of the potter's art – an aspect that continues to lie at the heart of the Craft Potters Association.

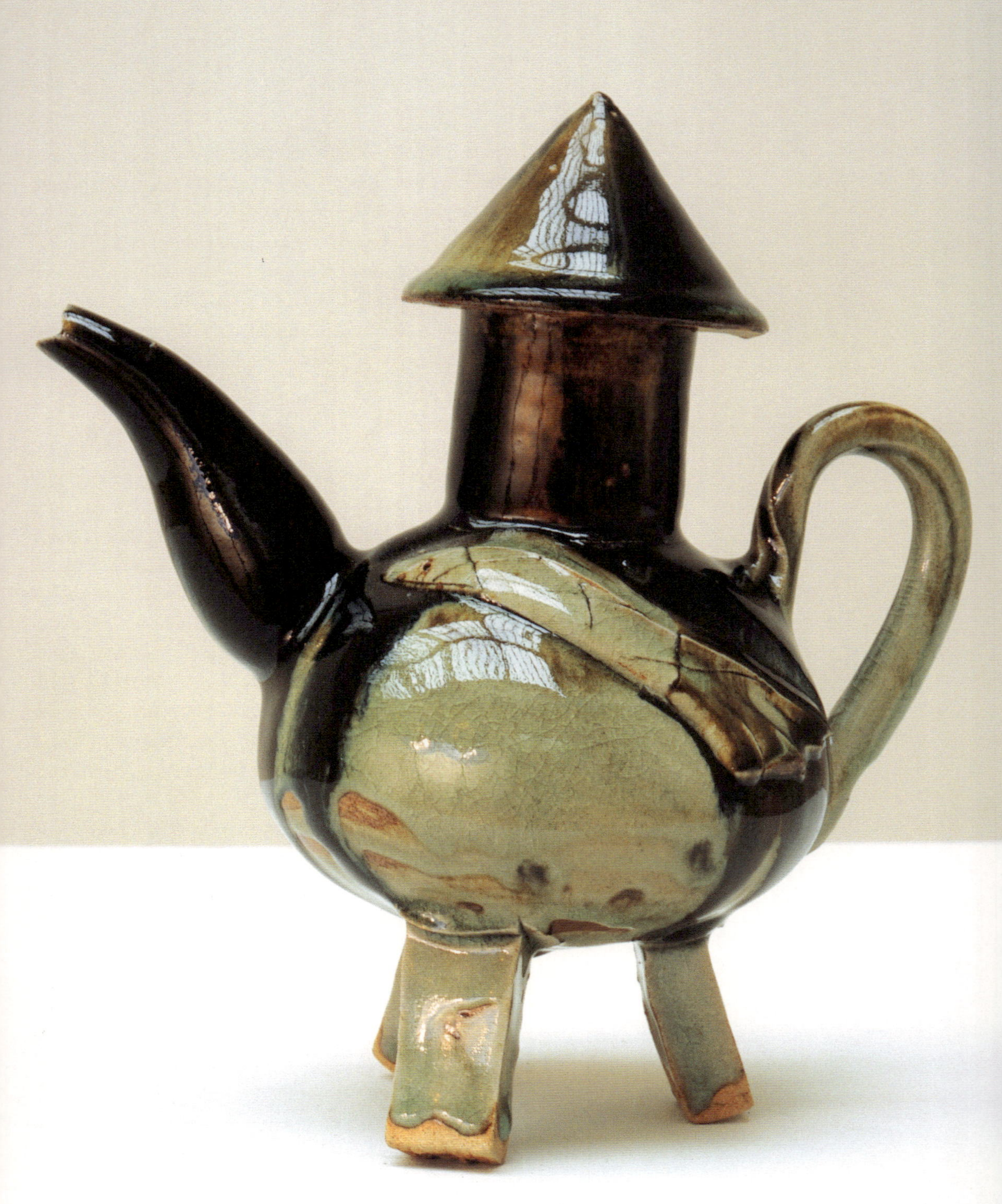

POT VESSEL OBJECT

by Emmanuel Cooper

"Since its inception fifty years ago, the CPA has fostered a spirit of community and co-operation"

◁ TERRY BELL-HUGHES
Fish Teapot, H20cm

* Paul Gauguin, title of his painting generally acknowledged to be one of his finest, completed 1897-8 and now in the Museum of Fine Arts, Boston.

An exhibition marking fifty years of showing, promoting and nurturing studio ceramics is a perfect opportunity to reflect on time past, time present and time future, and to ask big questions such as the ones posed by Paul Gauguin in the title of his masterpiece – 'Where do we come from? What are we? Where are we going?'*, a painting completed over a hundred years ago. While such immortal issues have no ready answers, they do open up intriguing areas for investigation, reflection and aspiration. As other essays detailing the first fifty years of the CPA in this book indicate, the organisation has a noble history; it knows, more or less, where it came from, the ideas that informed it and the people who helped give it shape. It can also make a fair assessment of where it is today, embracing commerce in maintaining a handsome retail gallery and shop in central London whilst also instigating a detailed education programme that includes fairs, talks and demonstrations and publications. The future is, as they say, another country. Doing the same or similar things more effectively, endeavouring to reach a wider audience and expounding the qualities of the handmade ceramic object are all important aspects that will ensure the CPA stays alive and responsive to market and ideological forces. Fifty years' experience offers a firm foundation from which to move forward.

▽ DAVID FRITH
Thrown Stoneware Platter, temmoku centre with ash glaze pouring, hakeme rim with ash, 2006, Ø50cm

▷ LISA HAMMOND
Soda Shino Vase, akebi handle and iron brush mark, 2007, Ø22cm

▽ CLIVE BOWEN
Large Wood-fired Platter, slip trailing, 2006, Ø56cm

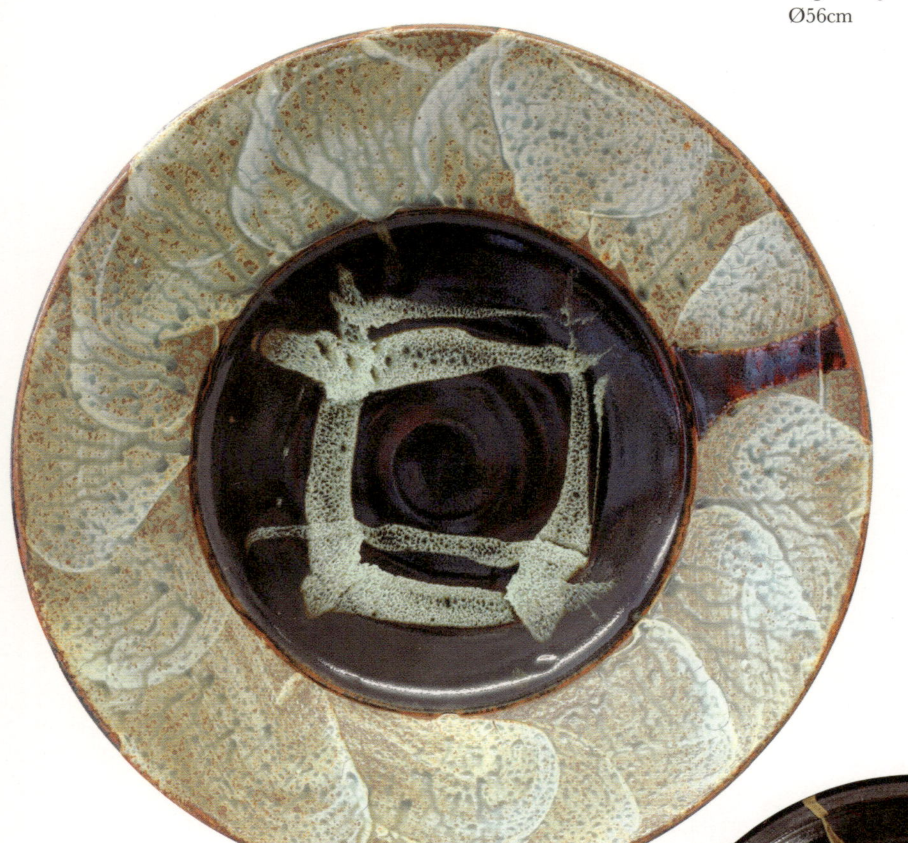

Since its inception fifty years ago, the CPA has fostered a spirit of community and co-operation in which potters and ceramists have sought to cultivate and encourage an art form they believe is truly expressive. It has looked for a set of shared values balanced with an acceptance that ceramics, like any other art medium, has many voices and can take many forms. Like long-established mutual building societies in which the investors own all the shares and strive for benefit for all rather than the few, the CPA has worked – and continues to work – for all its members, surviving financial and, occasionally, creative crises to become a reliable and trustworthy voice for a wide range of artists working with clay.

Against the necessity to survive financially, there have been other concerns that the CPA has addressed in the past and no doubt will continue to debate in the future, such as, for instance, the relative

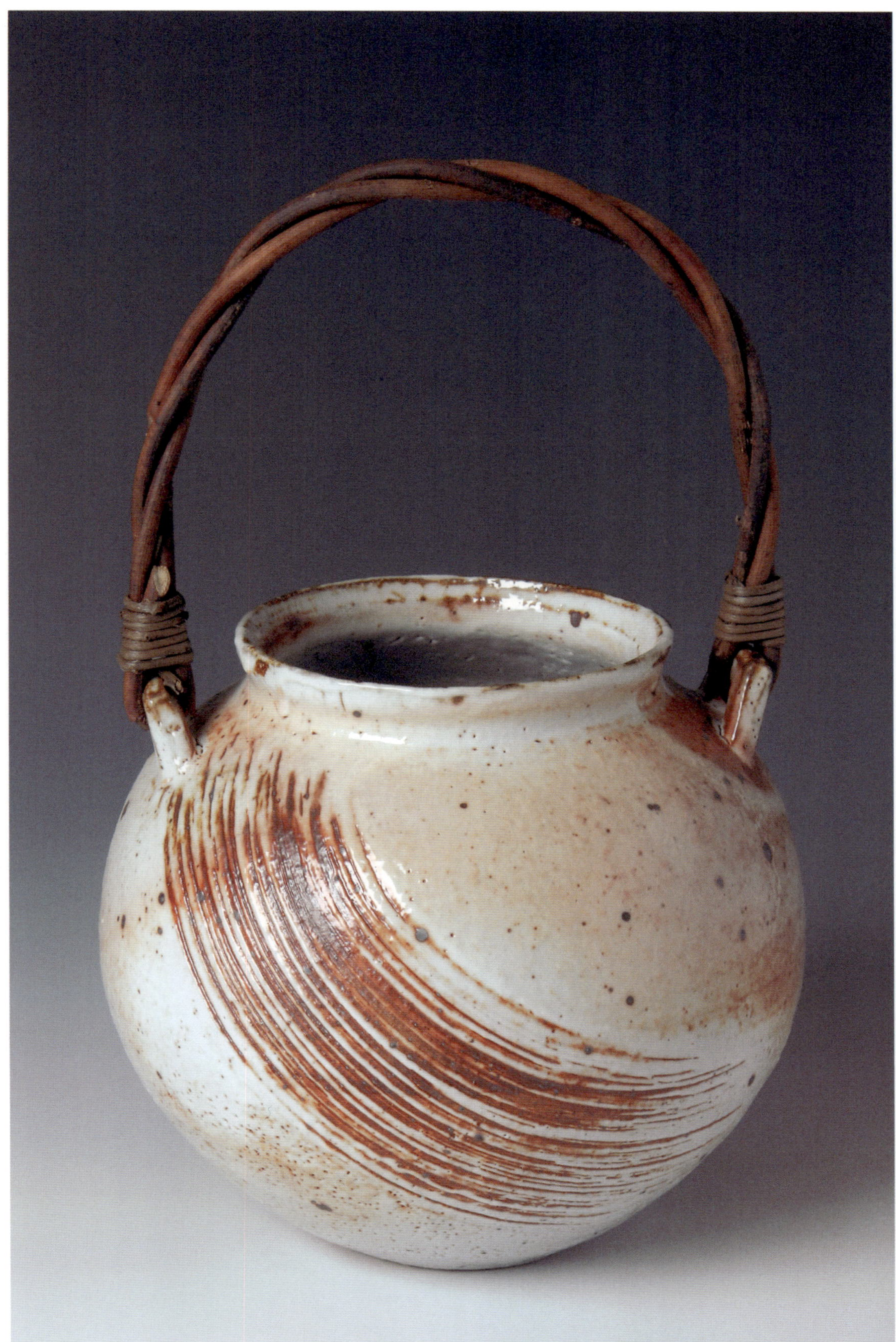

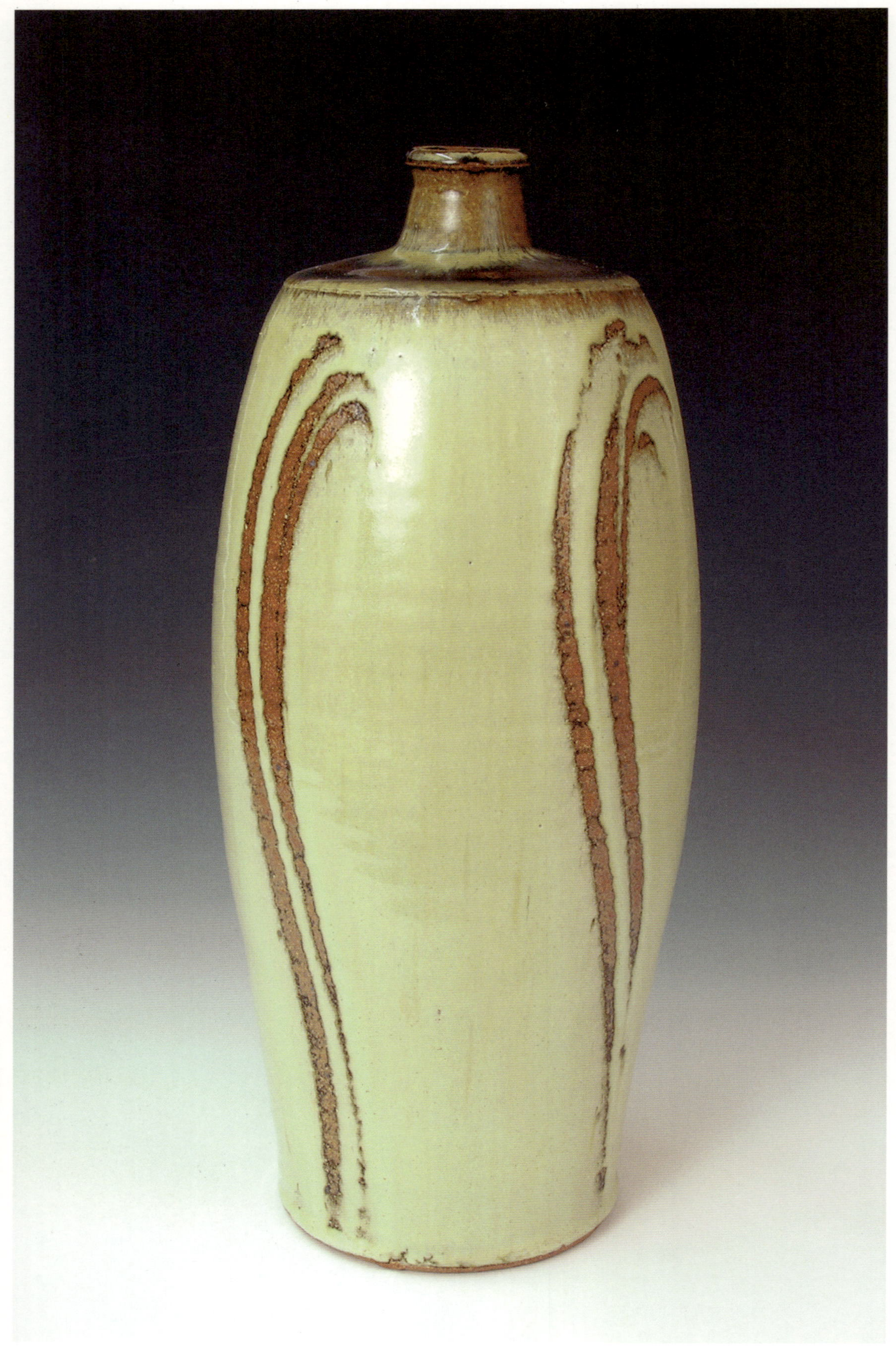

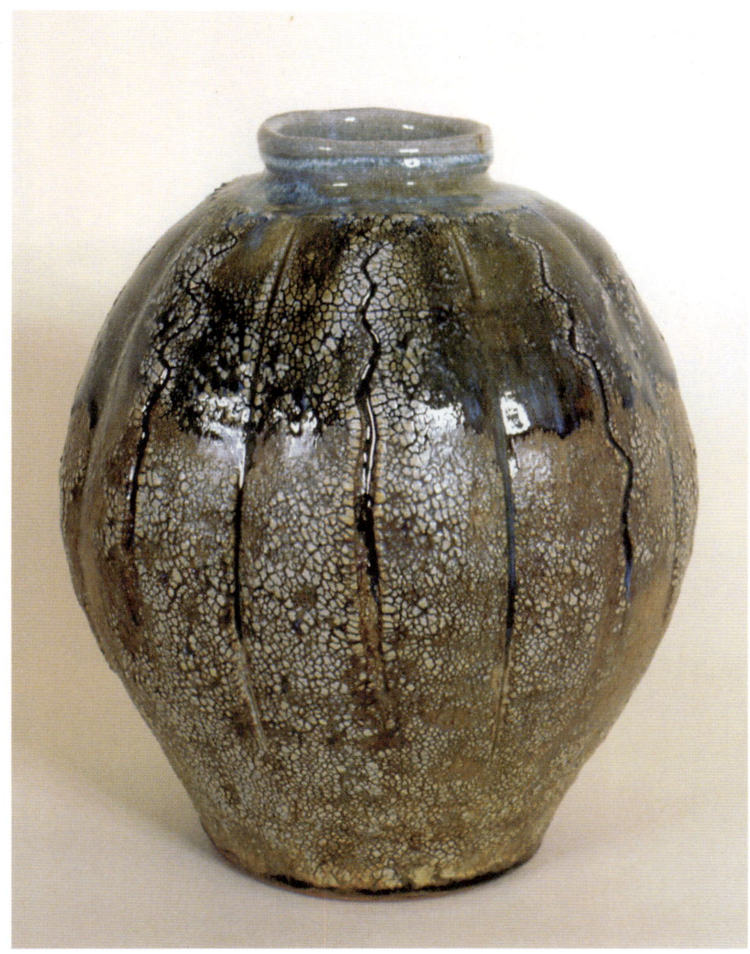

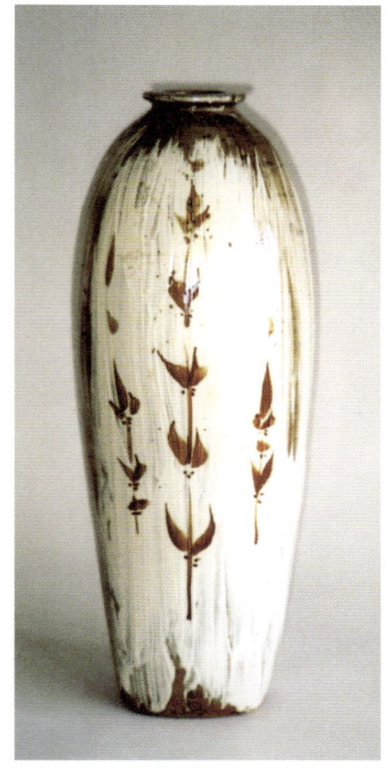

△ MIKE DODD
Textured Vase, expanded dry slip application, reduction firing, two ash glazes, 2006, H28cm approx

▷ JIM MALONE
Bottle, brushed slip, iron painting, H58cm

◁ PHIL ROGERS
Tall Bottle, nuka glaze and finger-wiped decoration, 2007, H37cm

values of the pot as against the vessel and the object. Between the useful and the useless. Between the ceramics that are washed and those that are dusted. Such debates, echoing the struggles between the representational and the non-representational in painting and sculpture, are the lifeblood of any co-operative organisation, striving to accommodate a broad spectrum of ideas and practices.

Yet, for all its history, it is vital that institutions such as the CPA respond to and initiate change. With fifty years of baggage and long-established ways of working, the readiness to react to shifting notions of what is worthwhile and important and what is not, whilst at the same time maintaining the value and importance of the handmade object, is a continual challenge. *The Pot, the Vessel, the Object*, which features the work of over forty current members of the organisation, is both a response to the history of studio ceramics in reflecting all its diversity

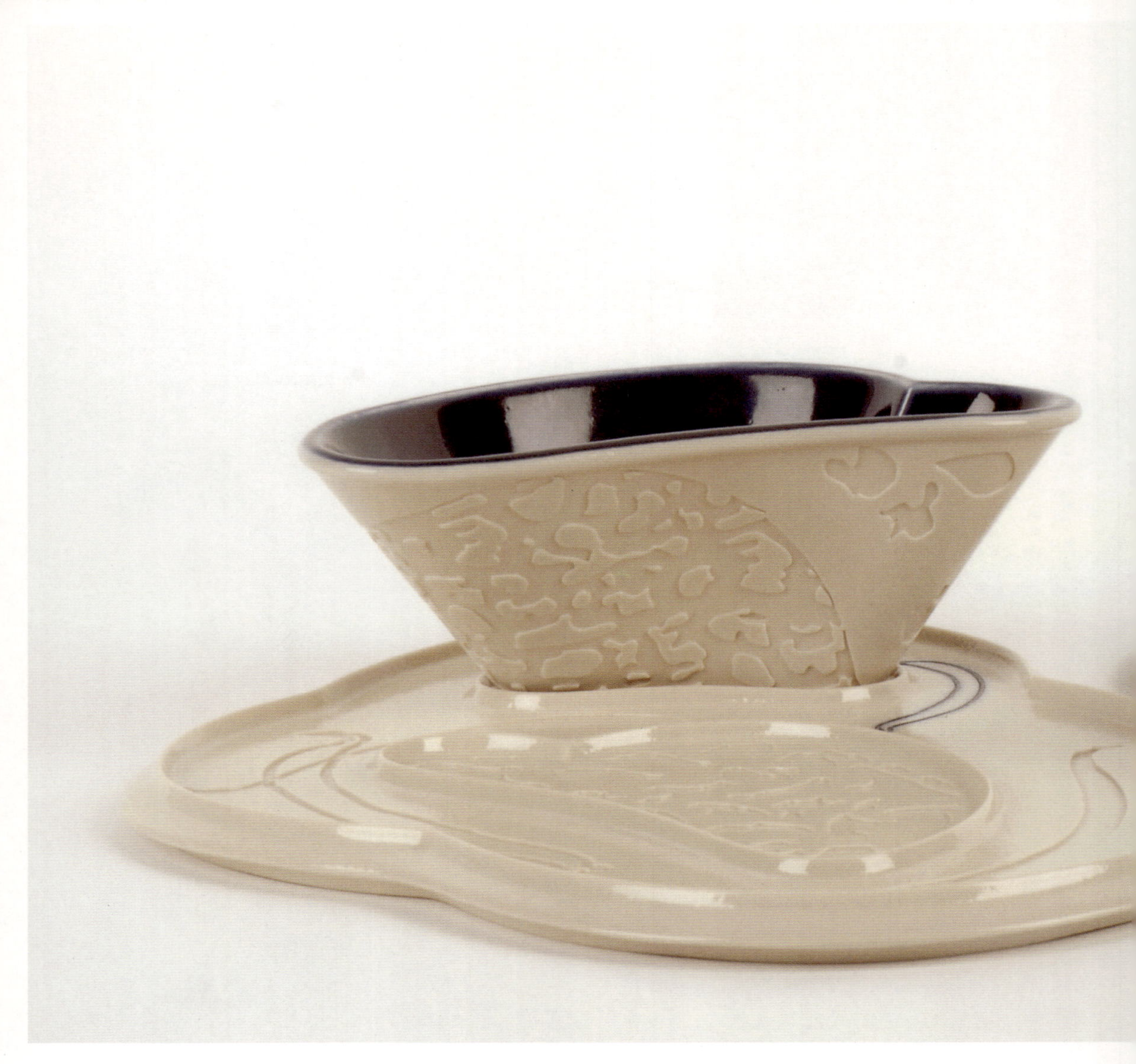

"The pots intended for use, to use Oliver Watson's defining phrase, can be seen as the 'ethical pots', pieces that combine use with beauty"

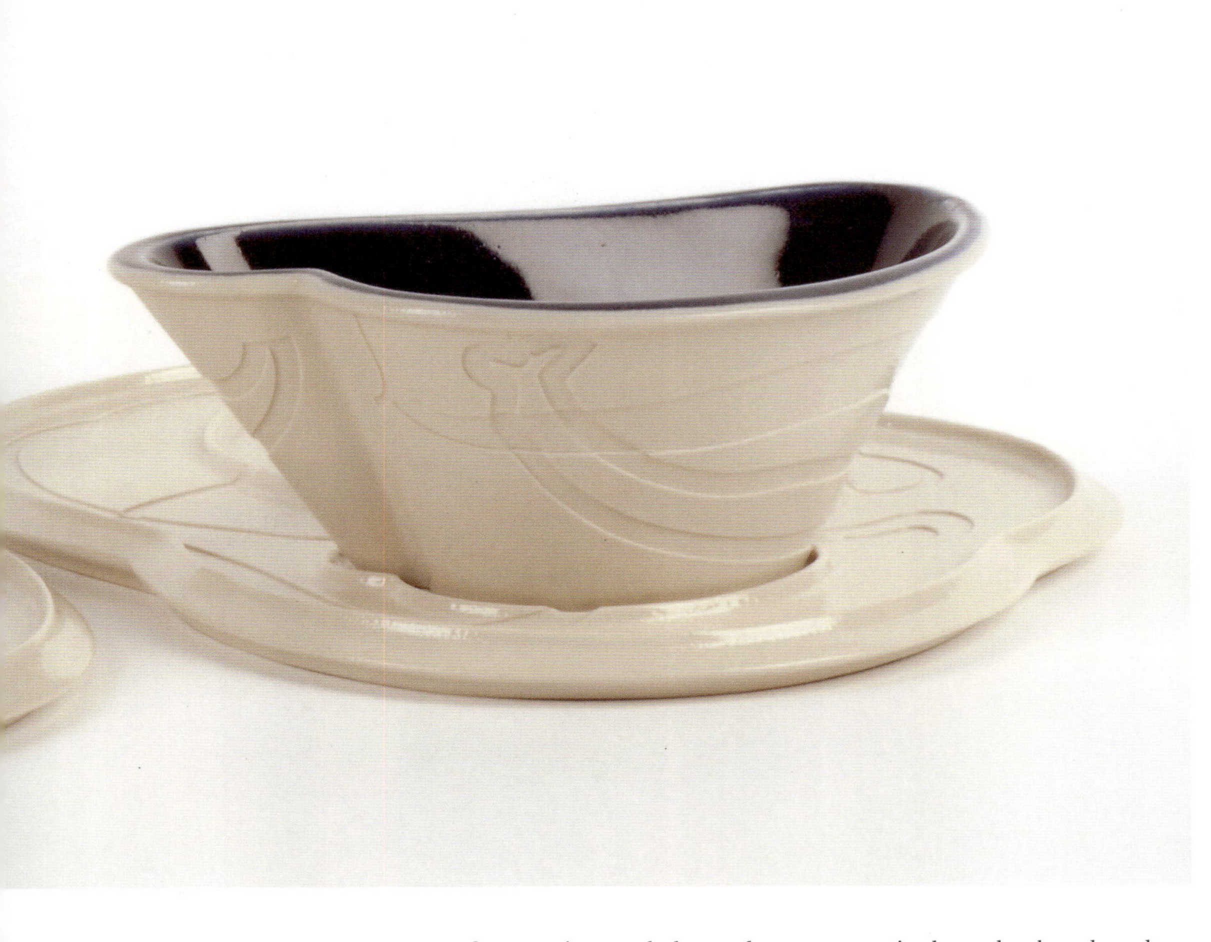

△ MORGEN HALL
Two Soda-Fired Porcelain Dish and Reversible Plate Sets, 2006, H6cm (Photo: Charles Aithie)

* Oliver Watson, *British Studio Pottery: The Victoria and Albert Museum Collection*, Phaidon/Christie's, London, 1990

of expression, and also to the way ceramics have developed, and are continuing to develop.

Even a brief glance at the history of studio ceramics in the twentieth century reveals an involvement in the pot as useful, something that may have a place in the kitchen, on the table or in the gallery. The pots intended for use, to use Oliver Watson's defining phrase, can be seen as the 'ethical pots'*, pieces that combine use with beauty. As early as 1900 Reginald Wells was making functional slipware in red earthenware with decoration in white clay in forms inspired by traditional seventeenth century Wrotham ware, although he later went on to produce high fired stoneware. From 1920 Bernard Leach and his student Michael Cardew (both of whom were later to become members of the CPA) produced useful pots as well as more decorative pieces. Leach, inspired by the ideas of William Morris as

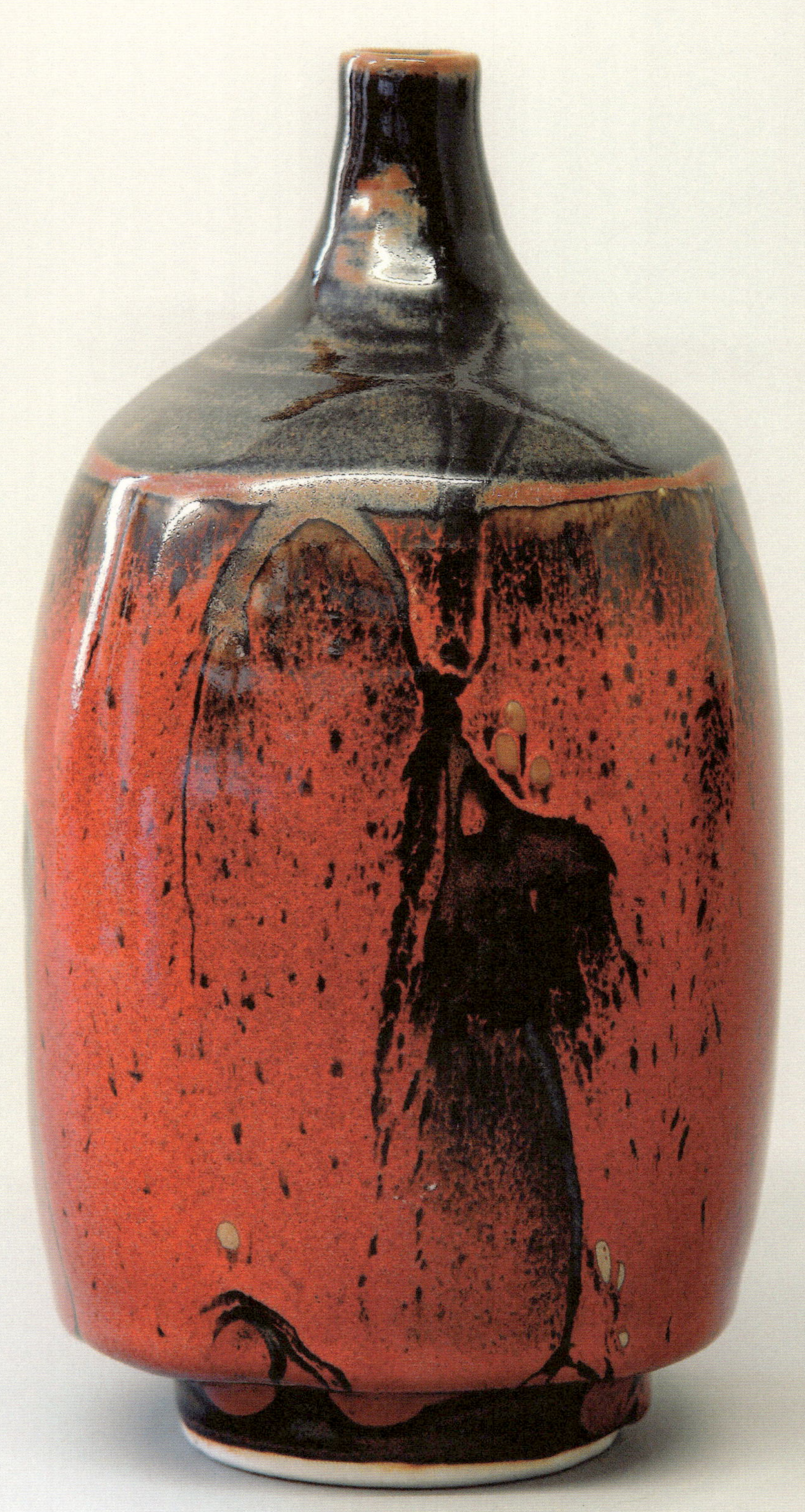

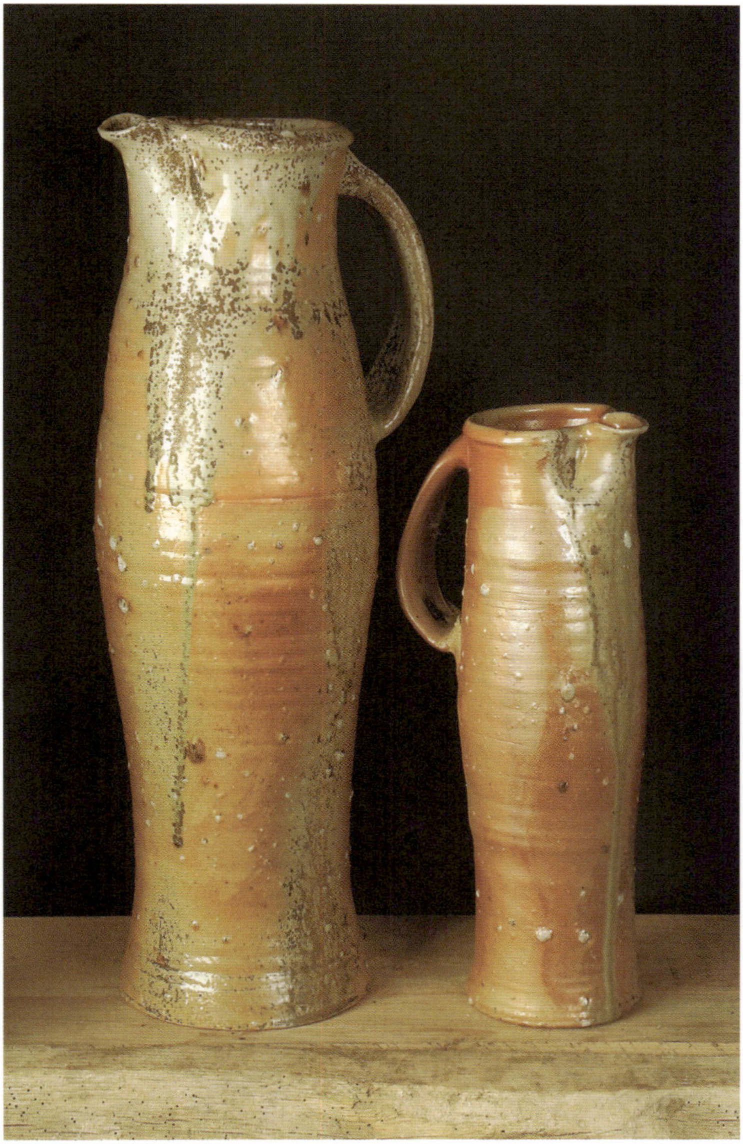

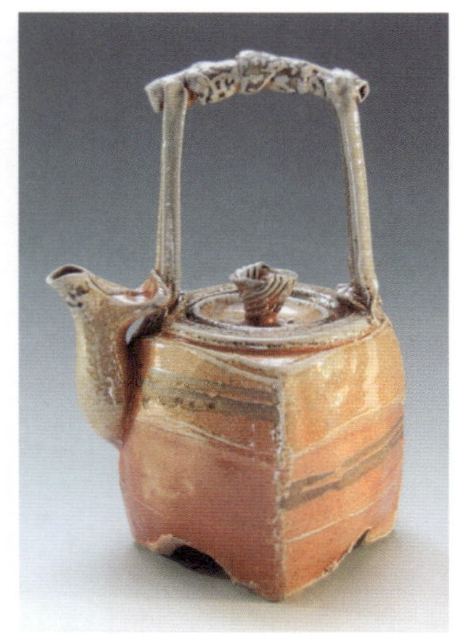

△ NIC COLLINS
Two Jugs, wood-fired stoneware, shino glaze with natural ash, 2005, H70cm max

▷ RUTHANNE TUDBALL
Bamboo Teapot on Four Feet, stoneware, soda vapour glazed, wood/gas fired, 2007, H23cm

◁ MARGARET FRITH
Squared Porcelain Bottle, temmoku glaze with wax motif and copper red glaze, 2007, H23cm

well as Zen Buddhism, enshrined the concept of the useful pot as a significant part of his practice, producing both tableware (though he himself rarely made it) alongside one-off or individual pieces that were intended as objects of contemplation. It was a way of working that served as a model, inspiring potters in this country and abroad throughout the century. For many potters it is still a satisfying method of working.

Leach's contemporary William Staite Murray took a different view. Although working in ceramics, Murray had no inhibitions about considering himself a fine artist and distanced himself from what he saw as the folk craft attitudes of Leach. Like Leach, Murray looked to the East, in particular to the stonewares of China and the ideas of Buddhism, as a source of inspiration. To follow Oliver Watson's

▷ CHRIS KEENAN
Temmoku Teapot and Two Cups with Rusty Spots, Limoges porcelain, 2005, H18cm

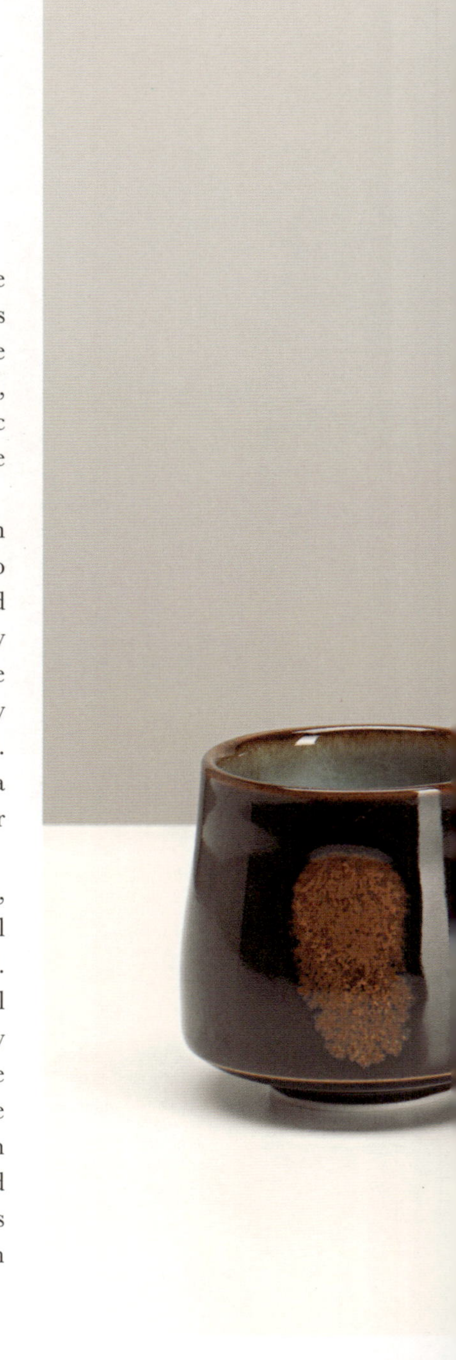

definition, Murray can be seen to represent the maker of the 'expressive pot', an object freed from any obligation to address anything but itself. One of the difficulties with this concept is that the 'ethical' pot, just like the 'expressive' pot, can be highly meaningful, capable of encompassing both use and beauty, achieving an aesthetic quality in which any reference to function heightens the sheer pleasure of the piece.

As Professor of Ceramics at the Royal College of Art, William Staite Murray taught many students, many of whom went on to become respected potters and teachers. Some became members and active supporters of the CPA in its early days, most notably Henry Hammond, Helen Pincombe and Paul Barron. In some ways all were vessel makers, whether building by hand (a method rarely used by potters making useful pieces as it is too slow) or throwing on the wheel. The term 'decorative' has been used to describe the work, but such a definition suggests surface qualities rather than depth, interior decoration rather than an 'expressive' quality.

The container, or the vessel, lies at the heart of much of the work, emotive words that in their brevity conjure up the conventional definition of a hollow receptacle, especially one that may be used. However, they do little to acknowledge the symbolic and metaphorical meaning of these engaging and humanistic forms. The dictionary definition of a pot, as might be expected, is broad, describing it in the simplest terms as a dish or container that is made from clay. There are no explicit references to the associations of the pot with use, which many of us are likely to assume. However, something that is labelled 'cooking pot', 'teapot' or 'fruit bowl', then as far as purpose is concerned, offers little or no ambiguity about its purpose – it has an

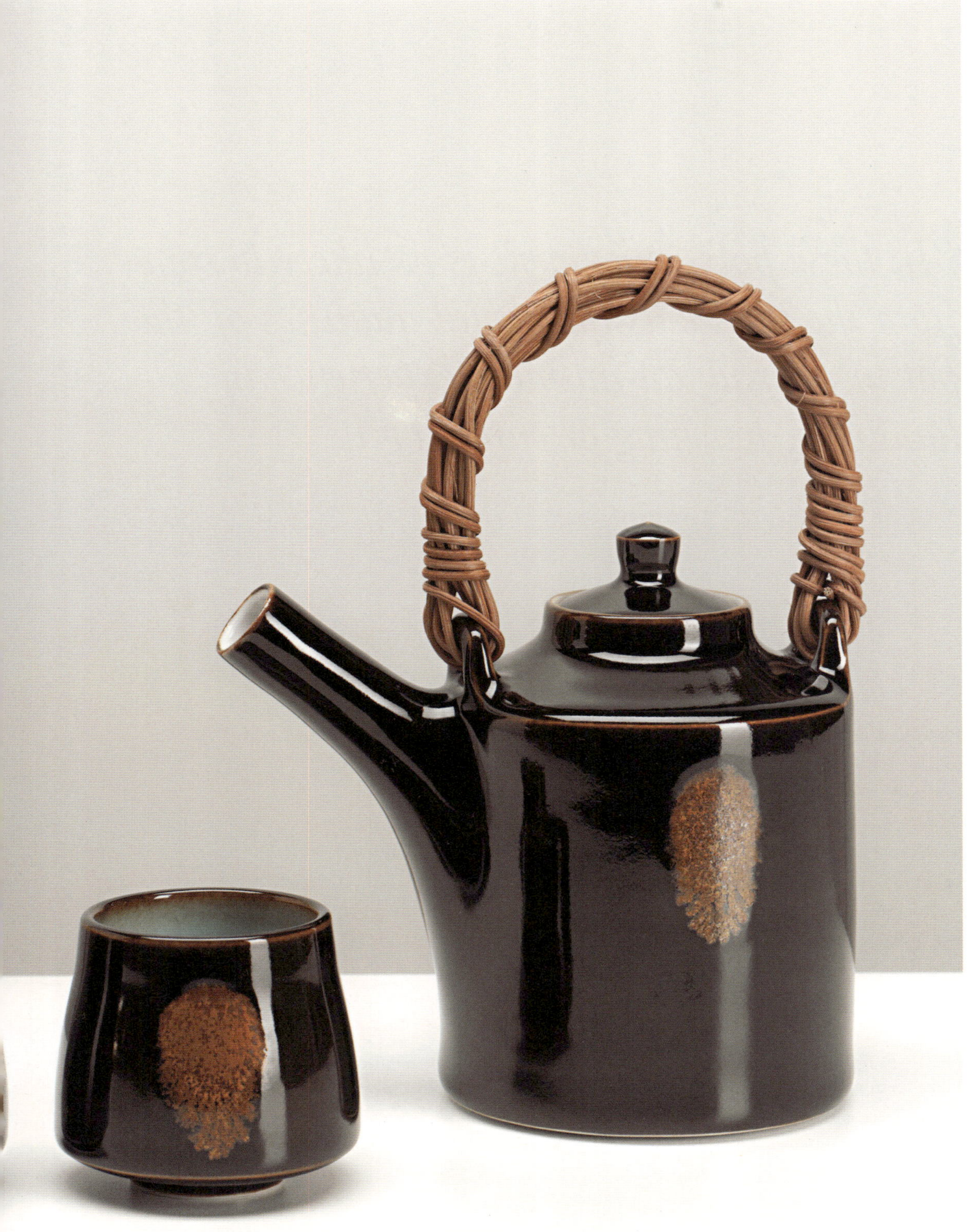

"In these pots, enjoyment is as likely to come from the tactile as the visual qualities of the pot in offering an intimate experience in handling, touching or caressing it"

identified and secure place in the domestic world. Although such labels make no reference to the possible beauty of the form or any symbolic role they may possess, this is left open to allow the viewer to deduce this for themselves. At least one of the aims of such pieces is to address the cooking-pot-ness, teapot-ness or fruit-bowl-ness – it is up to the user to decide if they succeed.

In these pots, enjoyment is as likely to come from the tactile as the visual qualities of the pot in offering an intimate experience in handling, touching or caressing it. Appearance will offer an initial attraction, but it is only when the piece is handled that enjoyment is fully realised. Who could resist employing the cool, pale blue porcelain pasta dishes made by Joanna Howells, with the unctuous glaze forming sensuous beads of colour on the strong forms? Equally alluring are the soda-kissed jugs and serving bowls made by Jeremy Steward, fired in a wood-burning kiln. The rich orange brown colour radiates reassuring warmth, making them ideally suited for a fine, nourishing meal. Chris Keenan, a city potter, approaches making tableware from a different point of view. His finely thrown teapots, bowls and mugs in porcelain covered with dark, mysterious temmokus and green-blue glazes, are both urban and urbane, as much about the hand of the potter as the eye of the designer. All,

▷ JEREMY STEWARD
Stoneware Jug, wood-fired, salt-glazed, 2007, H31cm

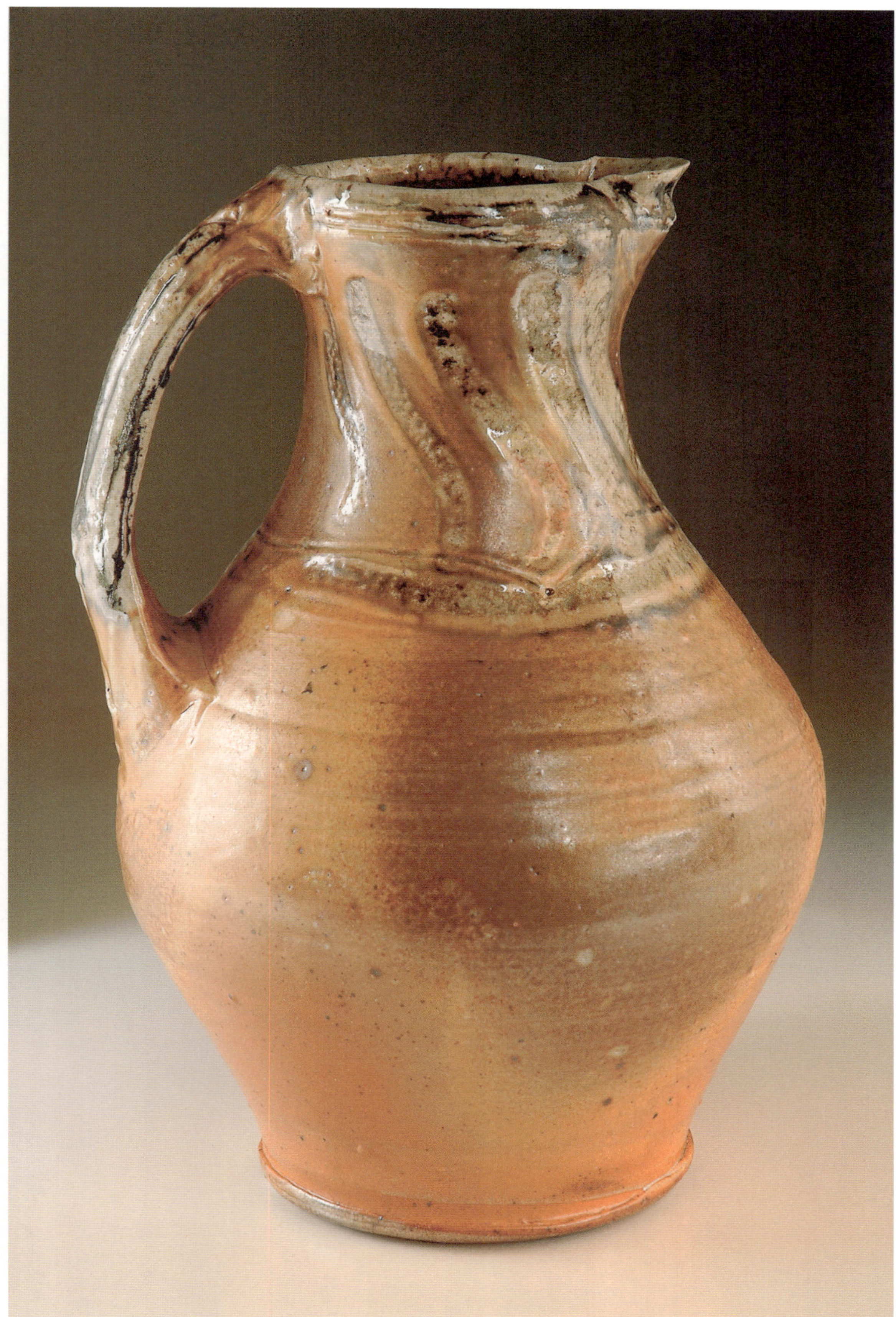

▷ MICKI SCHLOESSINGK

Group of Three Oval Teapots, 2007, H18cm

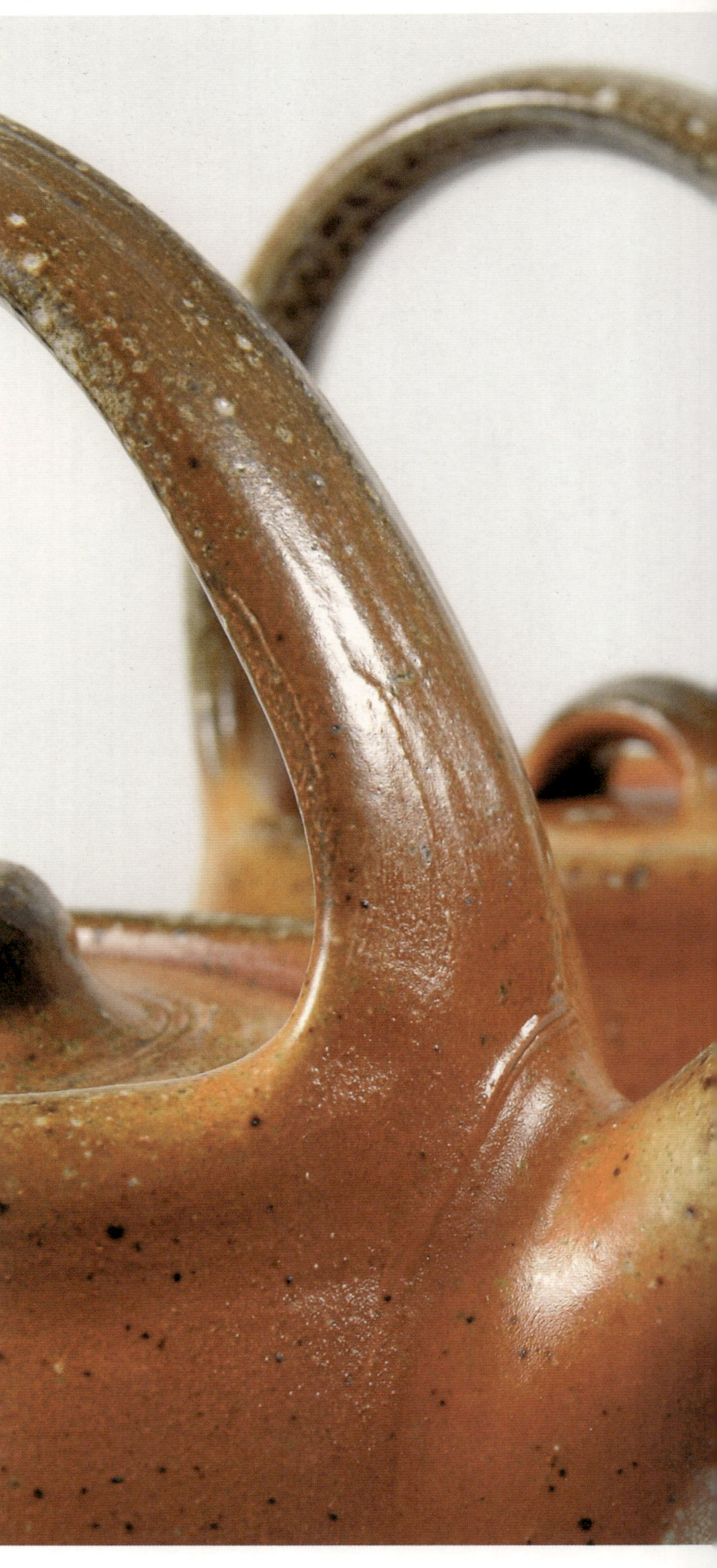

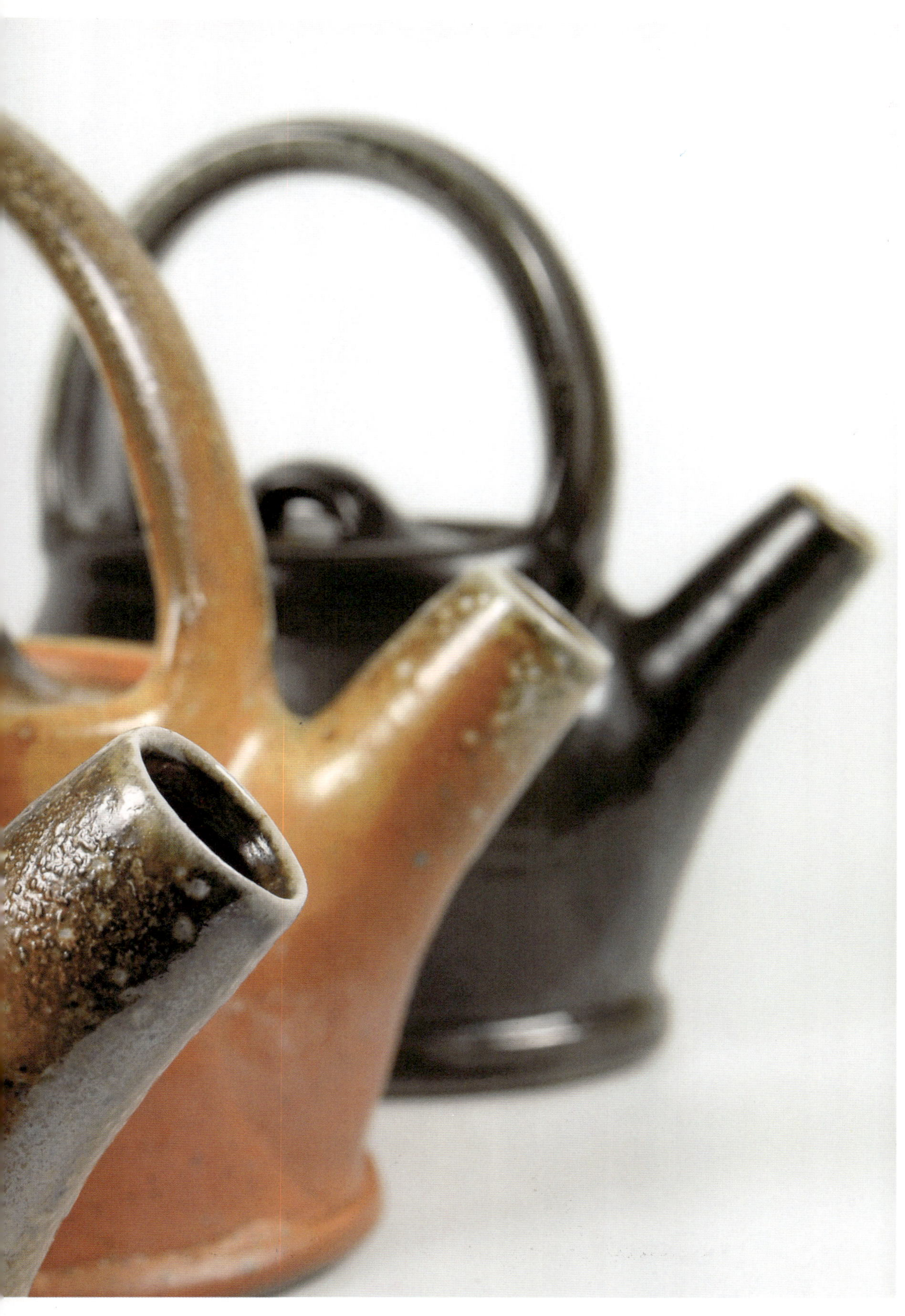

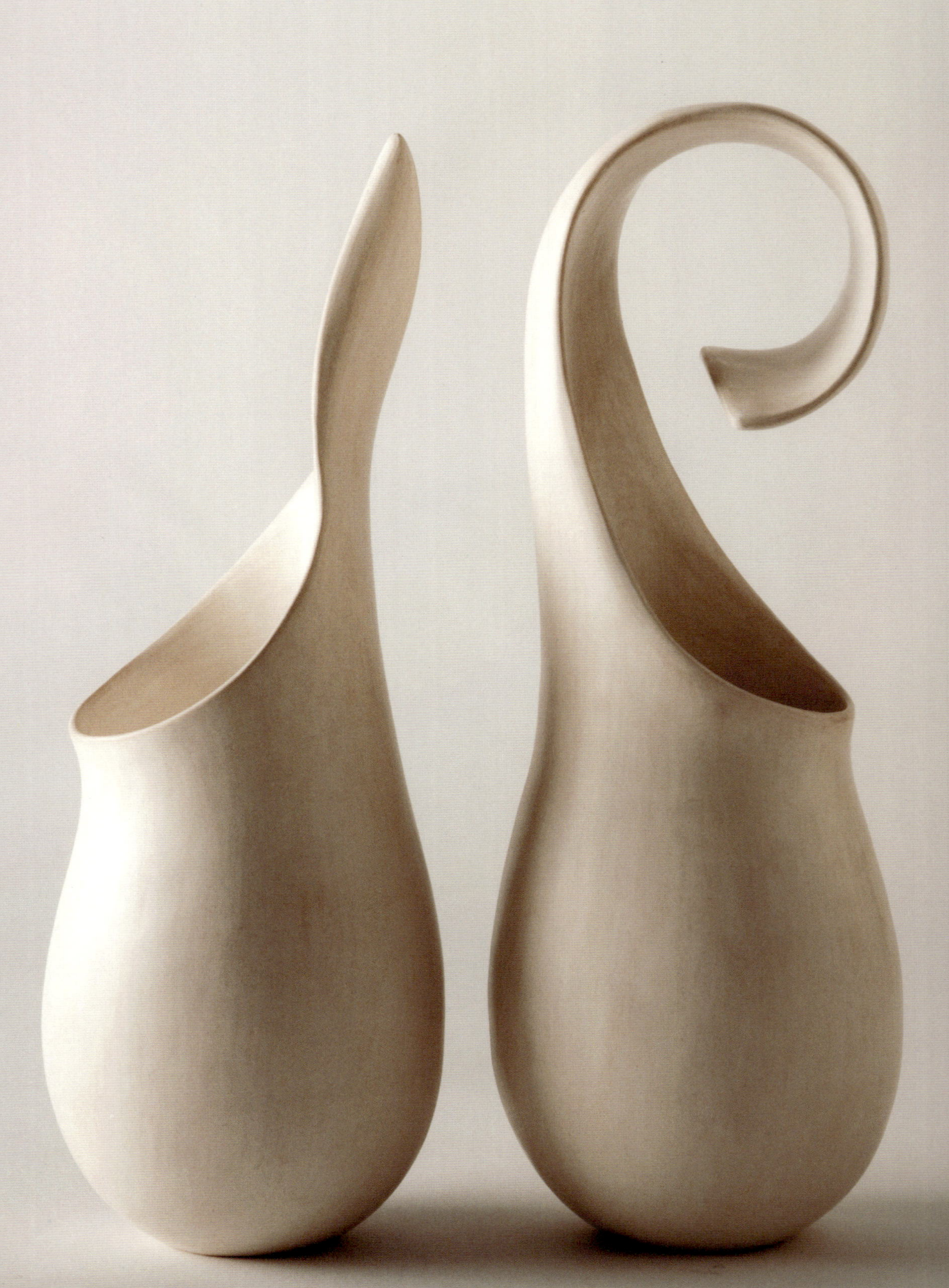

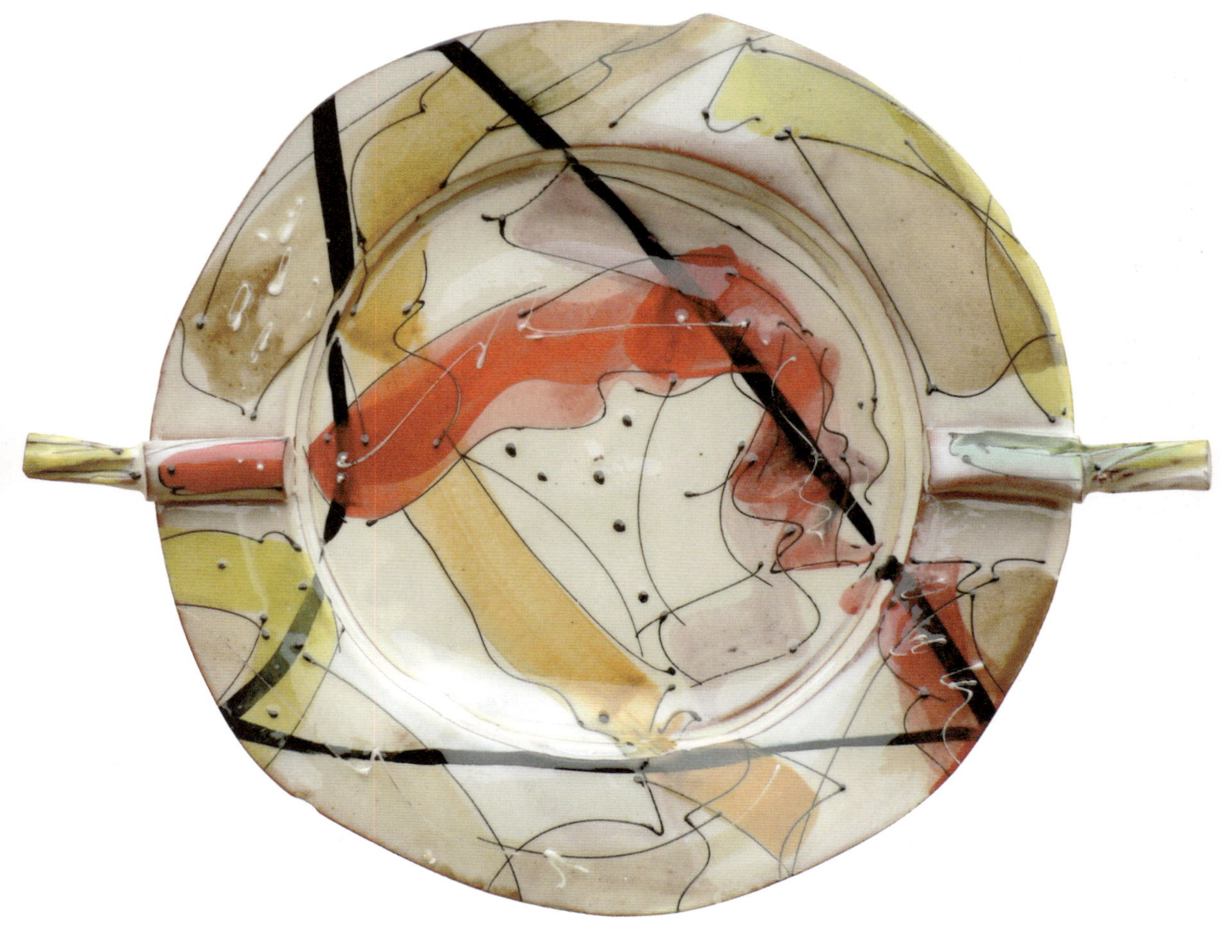

△ DAVID MILLER
Thrown Plate with Wire-Cut Handles, red earthenware with white slip, decorated with colour stains, fired to 1090°C, 2007, Ø43cm

◁ TINA VLASSOPULOS
Fin and *Curl*, burnished clay, 2007, H34cm max

however, make work that can happily find a place within the home and on the table.

Such work is unlikely to be described as vessels, though in all probability they are. In studio ceramic convention, objects defined as vessels are usually seen to have a distant, sometimes faint, relationship to use. Such work has appropriated and defined territory which, while retaining references to the container, may take on more metaphorical or symbolic qualities. In some ways they occupy the ground between the pot and the object, asserting their independence and authority with expressive work that has freed itself from any explicit function. They engage the eye and head through both idea and form. In a literal sense Tina Vlassopulos's delicately handbuilt forms are containers, but the rococo lines and the sumptuous curves defy any simple definition in terms of use but take us into new worlds in which meaning is fluid and open.

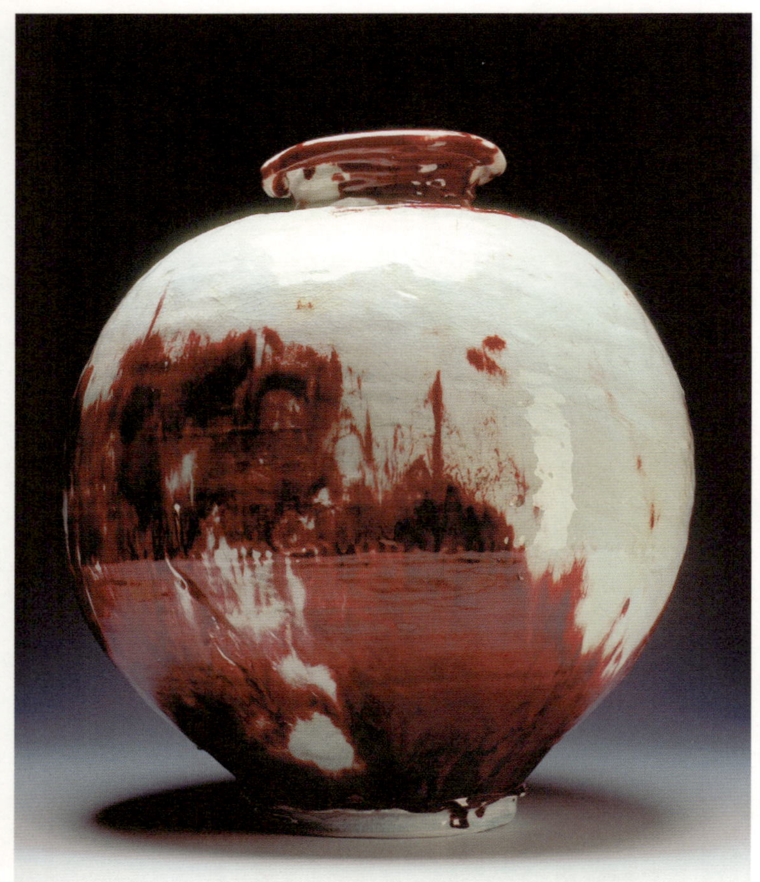

◁ GARETH MASON
Jar, stoneware, porcelain, slip, glaze, 2006, H66cm

▷ SIMON CARROLL
Jug, thrown red clay, slip decorated, gas fired, honey and tin glaze, 2006, H30cm

"Far from seeking to replicate in any sense the great classic exemplars, Gareth Mason pushes at the limits of form and firing, taking us to the edge in terms of process and ideas"

Who could dispute the engaging ambiguity of Simon Carroll's thrown and manipulated forms, be they jugs, beakers or bottles? Their origins may lie deep in the technology of English slipwares, but their psyche is very much of the twenty-first century. Look closely and it is possible to unravel the marks, decorative devices and their sources, all of which add to the multi-layered nature of the vessels. Working from a very different perspective, Gareth Mason draws ideas from other cultures, in particular those of the Far East, using reduction fired stoneware and porcelain to explore the qualities of the material and making process. But, far from seeking to replicate in any sense the great classic exemplars, he pushes at the limits of form and firing, taking us to the edge in terms of process and ideas. These, too, are rooted in today, and in the way we deal with the past and the present.

If the pot and the vessel pose problems in terms of definition, at least they share a concern based around the idea of the container, things with interior volume, pieces with walls that can be seen as defining and shaping. The object has no such limits and, in contrast to both the pot and the vessel, it has even fewer defining qualities, merely being described as something that can be seen or touched, a definition that applies to all three ceramic forms. While an object may be hollow, it is an interior that

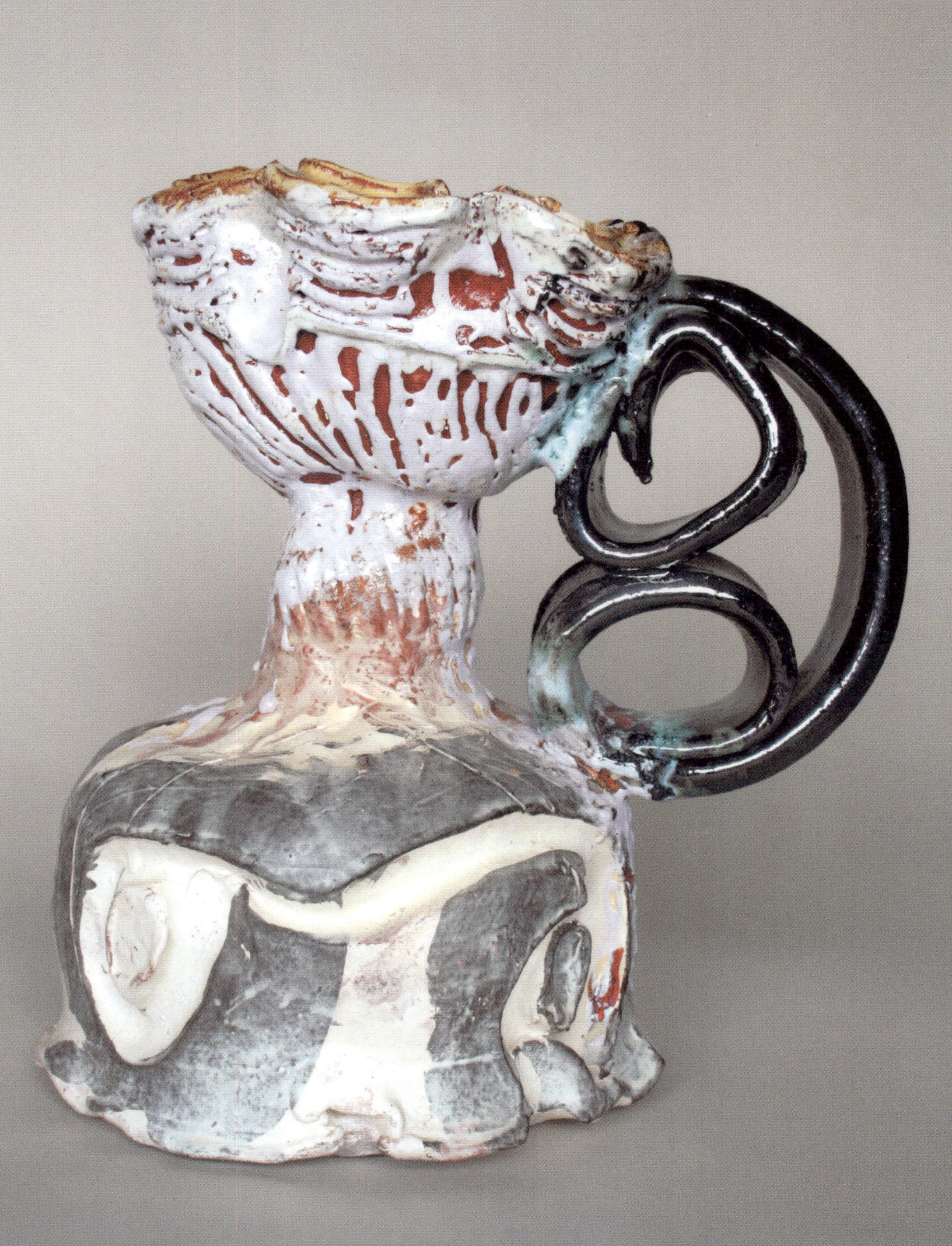

▷ SARAH WALTON
No. 4 Birdbath, salt-glazed ceramic on green oak wood base, 2006, W46cm

▽ LISA KATZENSTEIN
Three Tall Twist Vases, hand-painted maiolica, H45cm

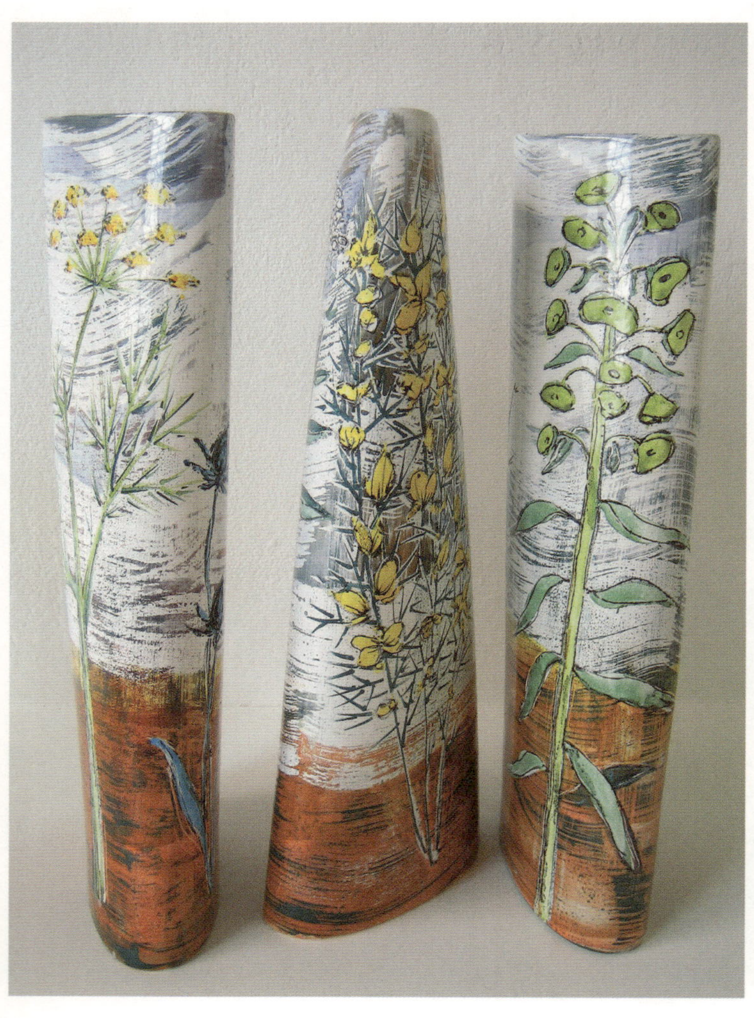

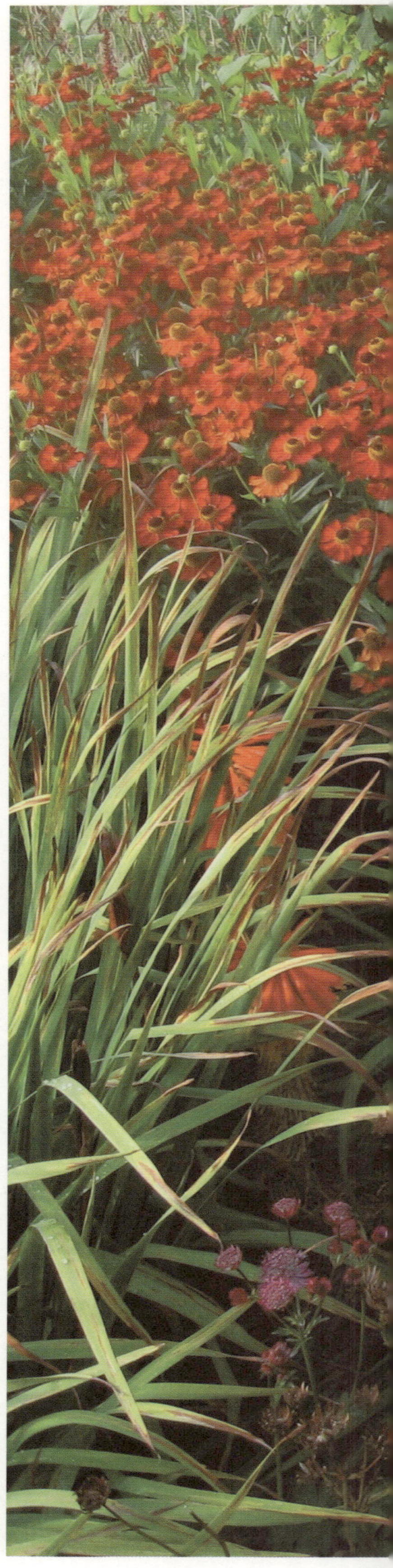

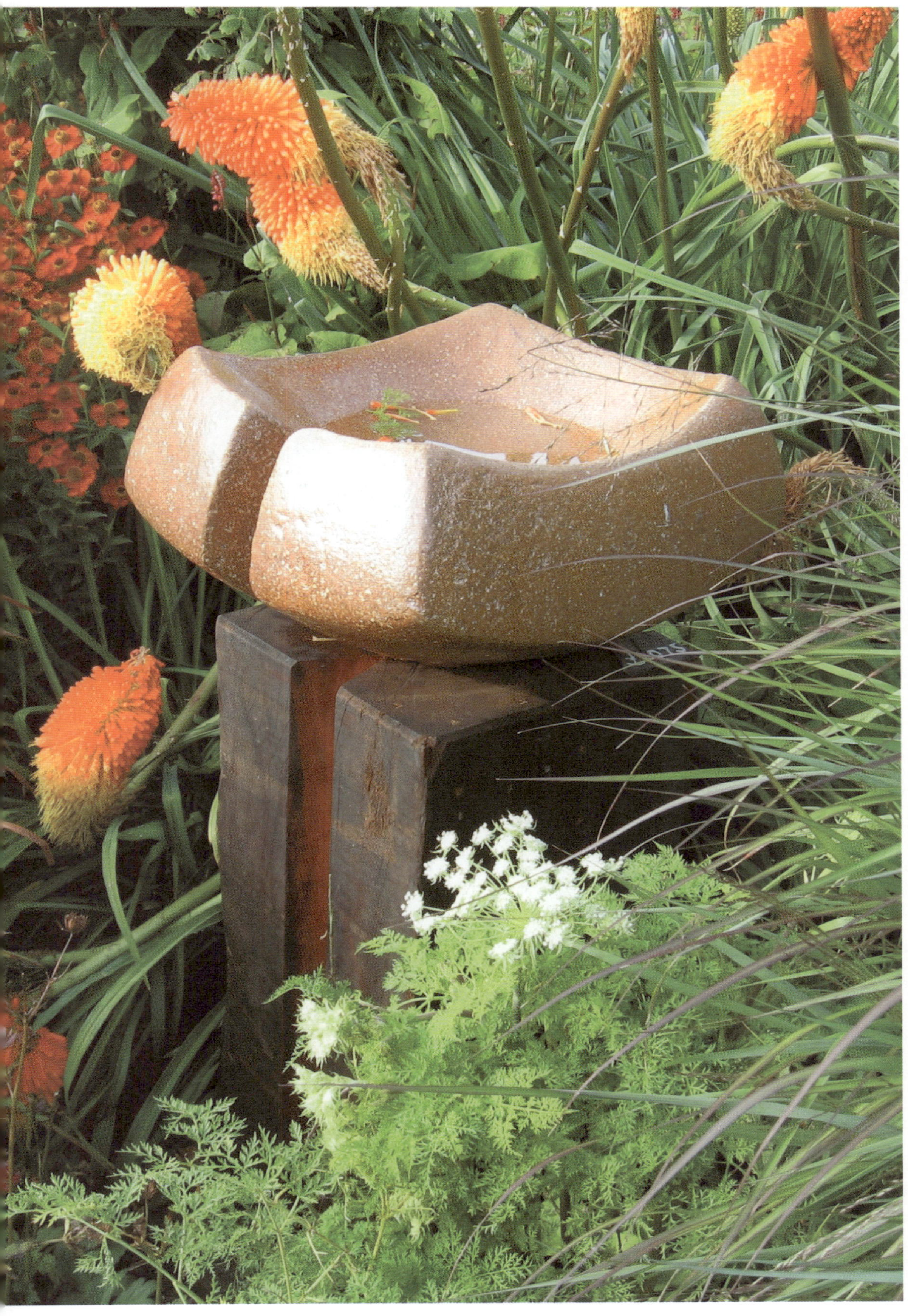

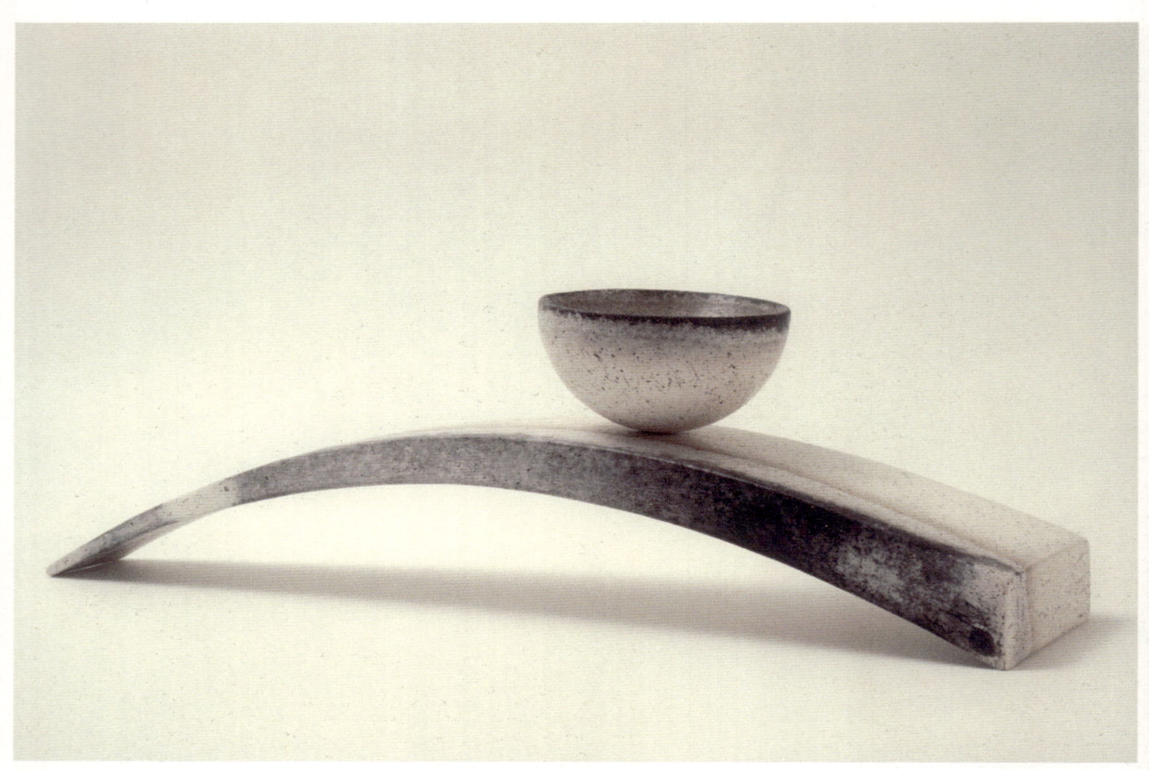

△ JANE PERRYMAN
Touching Balance, T material and porcelain, 2007, L44cm

▷ ANTONIA SALMON
Touch Point, smoke-fired white stoneware, 2007, H34cm

is completely enclosed, a space to which the viewer has no access. The object here is more likely to follow the 'rules' of sculpture in having an abstract concern with line, volume, space and possibly colour.

Here I am not referring to figurative work, which poses its own definitions, but to work that is purely non-representational, abstract in its concerns, though we may recognise references to the natural world or the built environment. These references are likely to be subliminal rather than explicit, as, for example, in the work of Peter Beard or the precisely crafted forms of Jane Perryman or Antonia Salmon. We can only view these as sculptural forms that open up debate on the inventive use of material and process and the play of light and shade whilst suggesting possible metaphorical ideas and allusions. They also embody intriguing qualities in which balance and counterbalance keep our eye and mind returning to them time and time again. The structure and the concept is defined entirely by the artist, working in tune with the processes they have chosen.

Yet to include all three in the title of an exhibition could be seen to imply some distinction between them, which directs the way we see and enjoy the work, indicating, perhaps, the differences between the aim of the artist and the perceptions of the viewer. Whilst the three contrasting descriptions suggests categories and implies separation, they are all part of a multi-layered whole in which one gains from the other.

To discuss such work using the language and aesthetic concepts of sculpture is appropriate. Yet, such language can usefully be applied to the

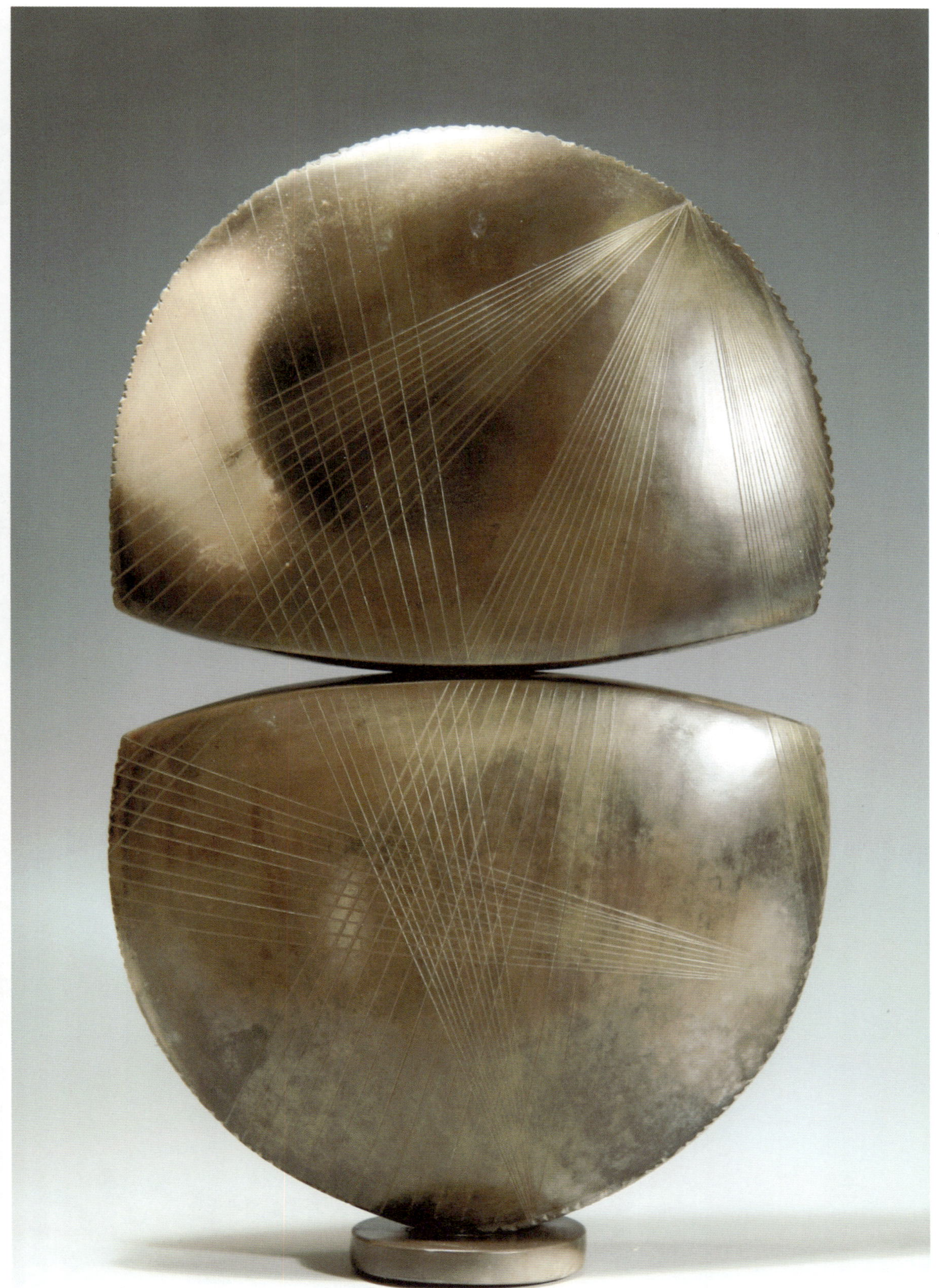

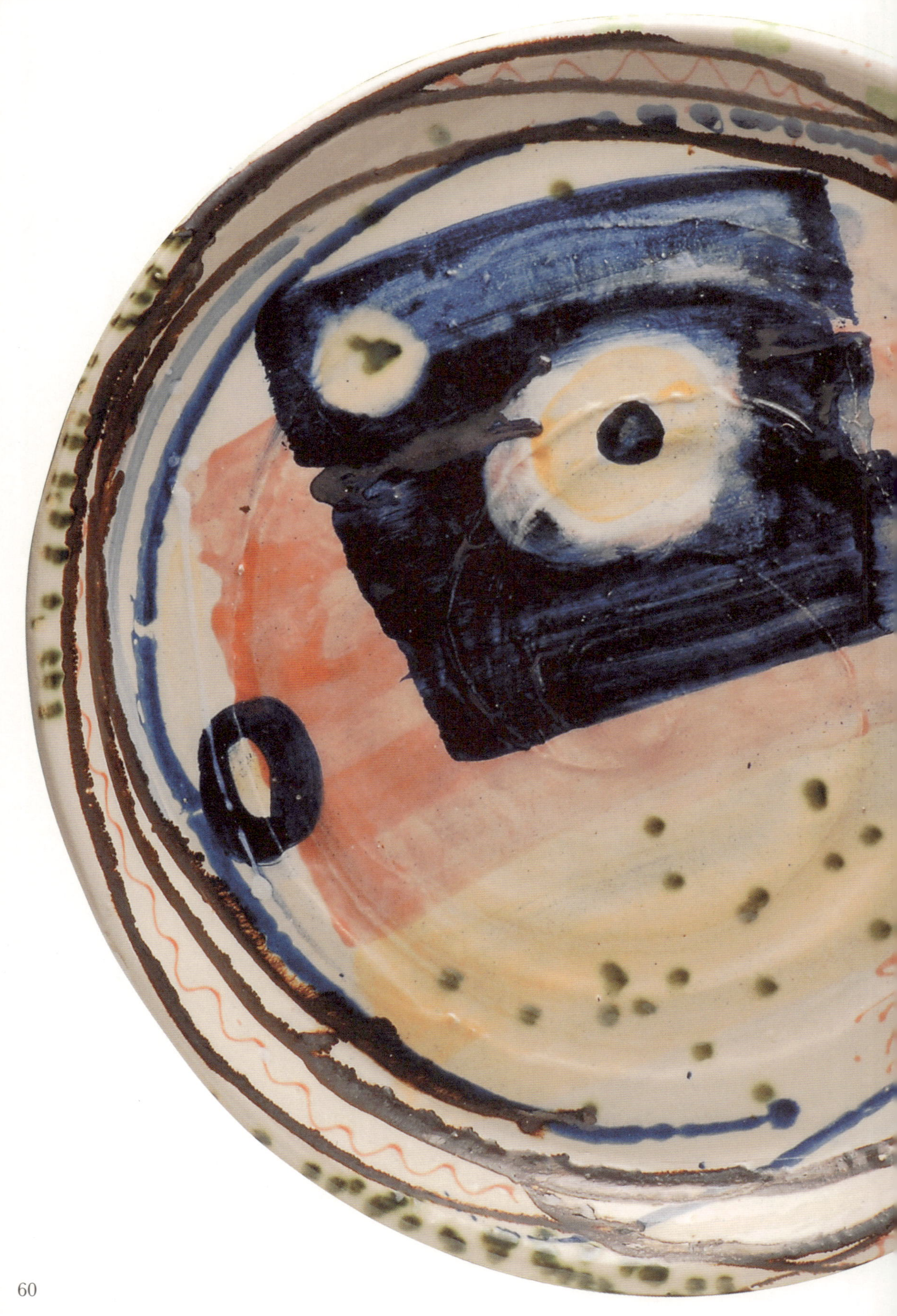

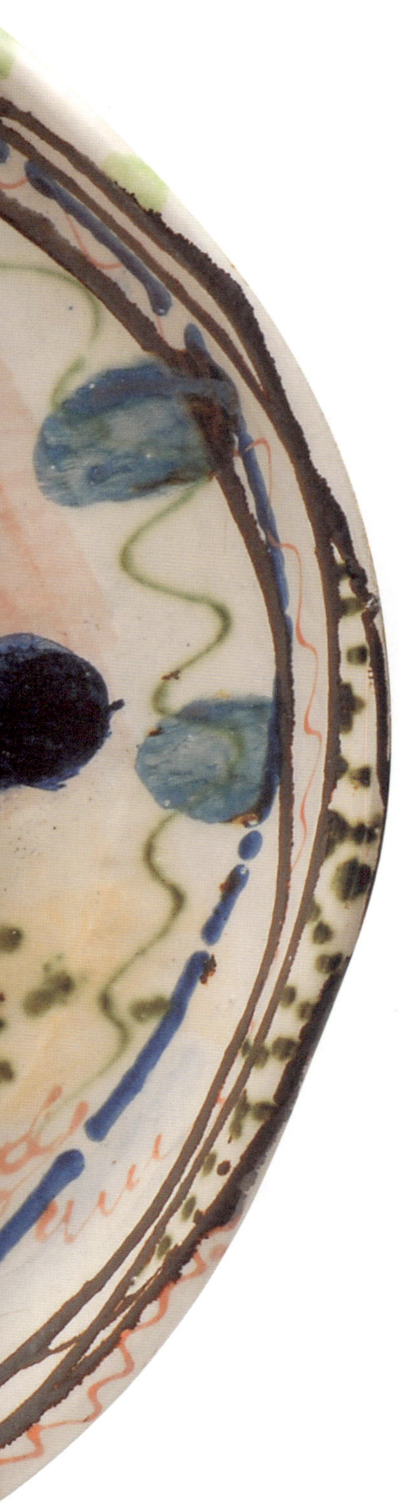

◁ SANDY BROWN
Softly Thrown Platter with Smudge,
stoneware, white slip, coloured glazes,
2005, Ø48cm

▽ PETER BEARD
Cut Form, oxidised stoneware with wax
resist glazing, on slate base, 2007, L23cm

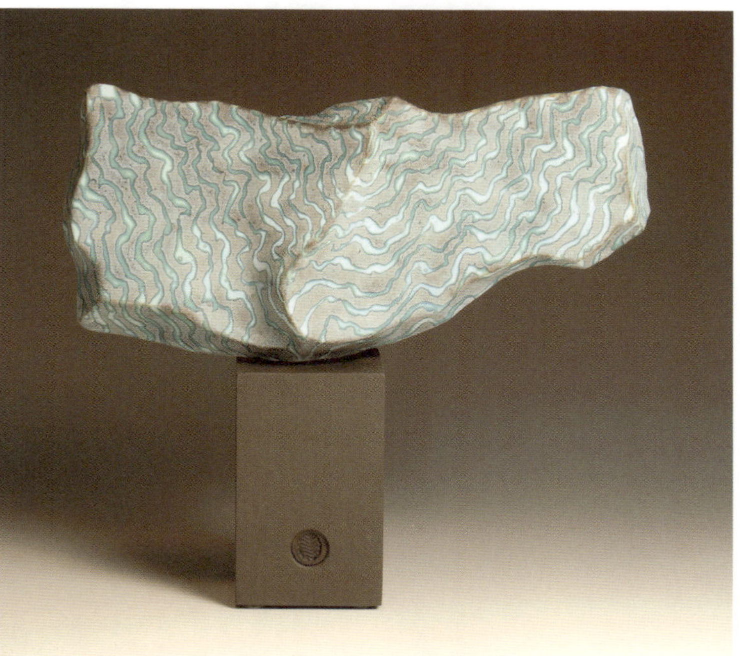

pot, the vessel and the object, acknowledging that the structure within which the artist is working may be narrower with more goals to achieve. Teapots must pour efficiently, cups need to be comfortable to hold and plates practical to use, objects must engage and retain our visual and mental interest. On the evidence of *The Pot, the Vessel, the Object*, while there is a sense of history and an acknowledgement of the past, there is also an awareness of and an engagement with the present; on the basis of this work there is a thoughtful and expansive future to be explored in which we have to decide whether we are looking at pots, vessels or objects.

"On the basis of this work there is a thoughtful and expansive future to be explored"

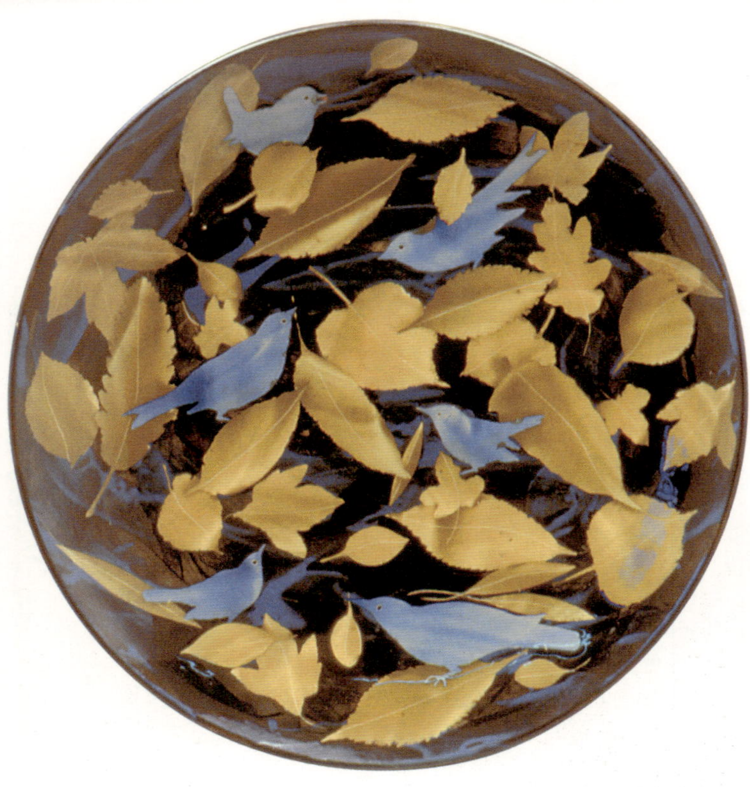

△ SOPHIE MacCARTHY
Bluebirds and Leaves, Ø38cm

▽ JACK DOHERTY
Ribbed Porcelain Bowl, thrown and soda fired, 2007, Ø35cm

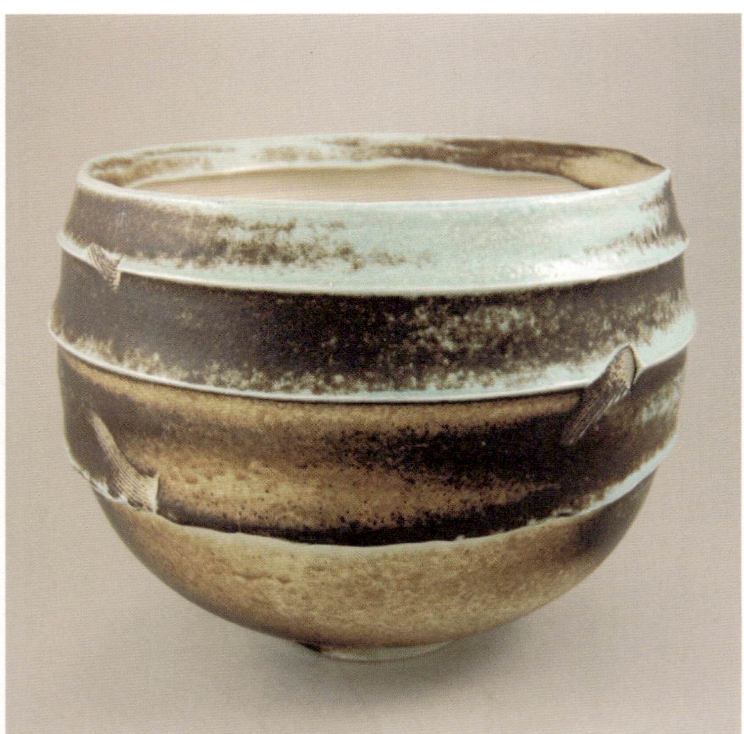

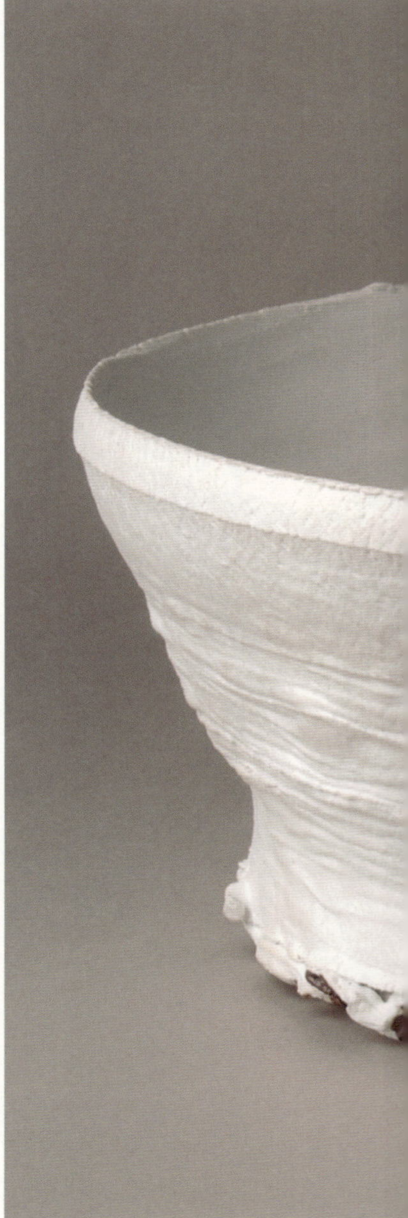

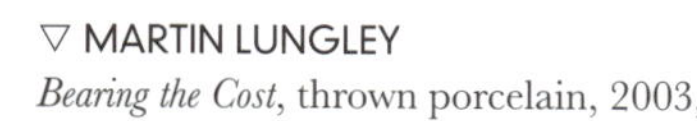

▽ MARTIN LUNGLEY
Bearing the Cost, thrown porcelain, 2003, H18cm

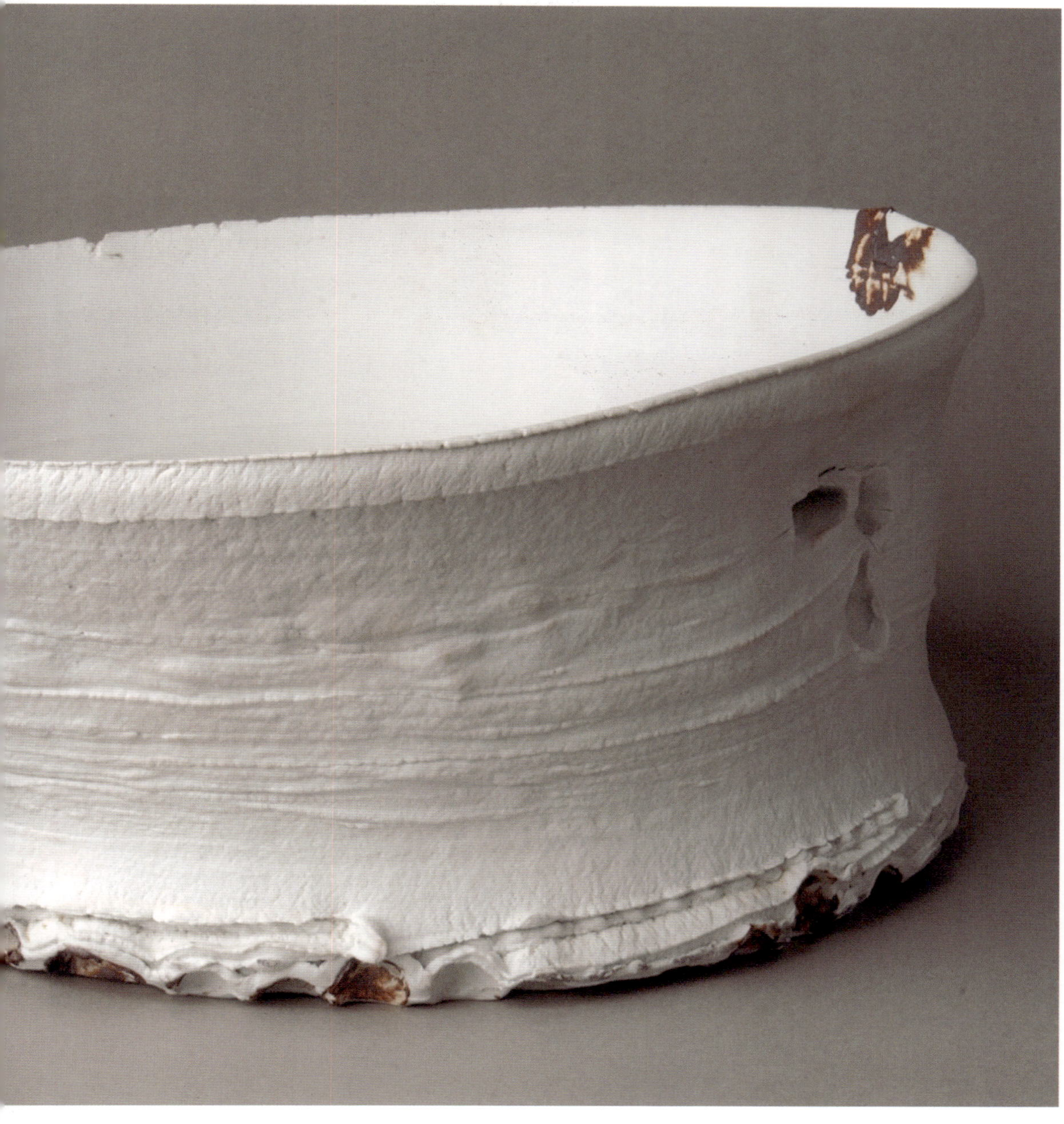

▷ BEVERLY BELL-HUGHES
Razer Wave, H18cm

▽ FELICITY AYLIEFF
Red and Acid Yellow Vessels, handbuilt, white stoneware clay, vitreous slip, 2006, H80cm

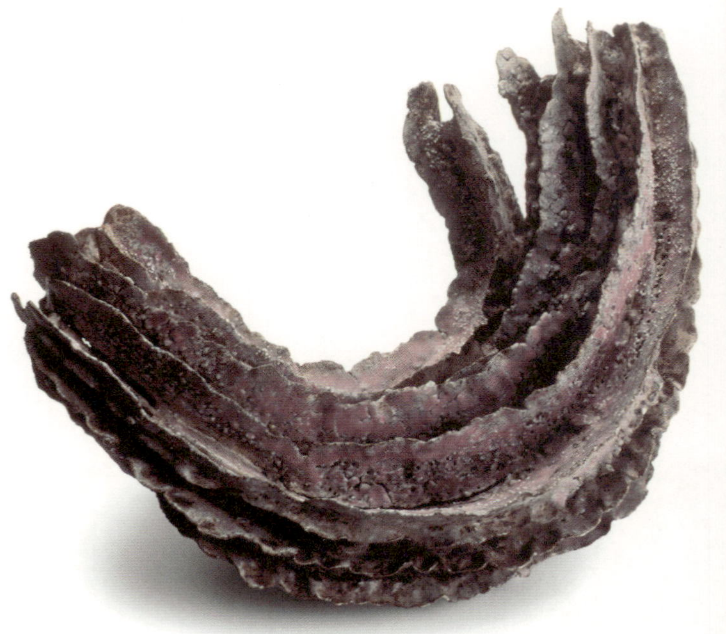

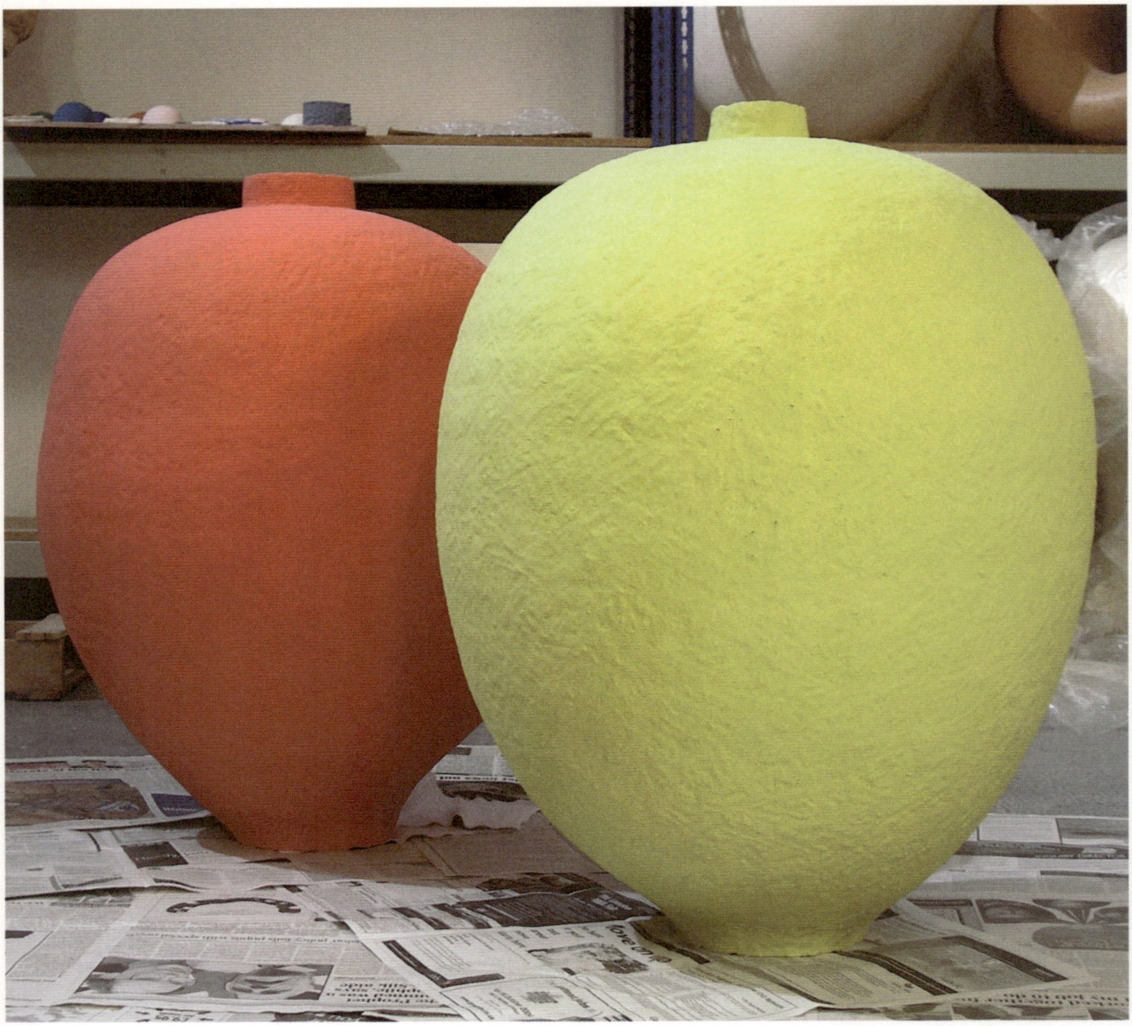

▽ JOANNA HOWELLS
Chthonic #1, porcelain, 2006, H31cm

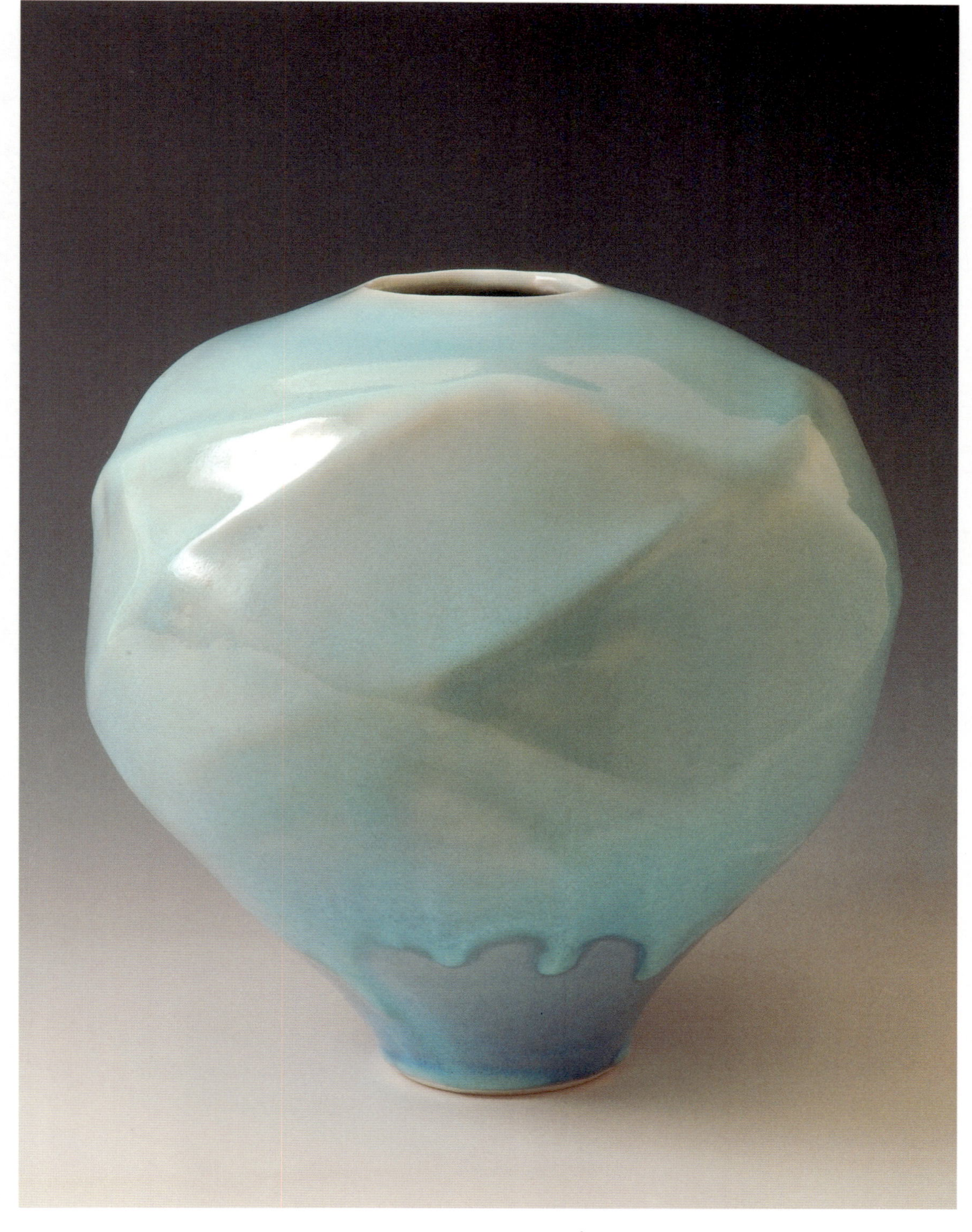

▷ MARTIN McWILLIAM
Small F-F Jars 1, 2 and 3, H21cm

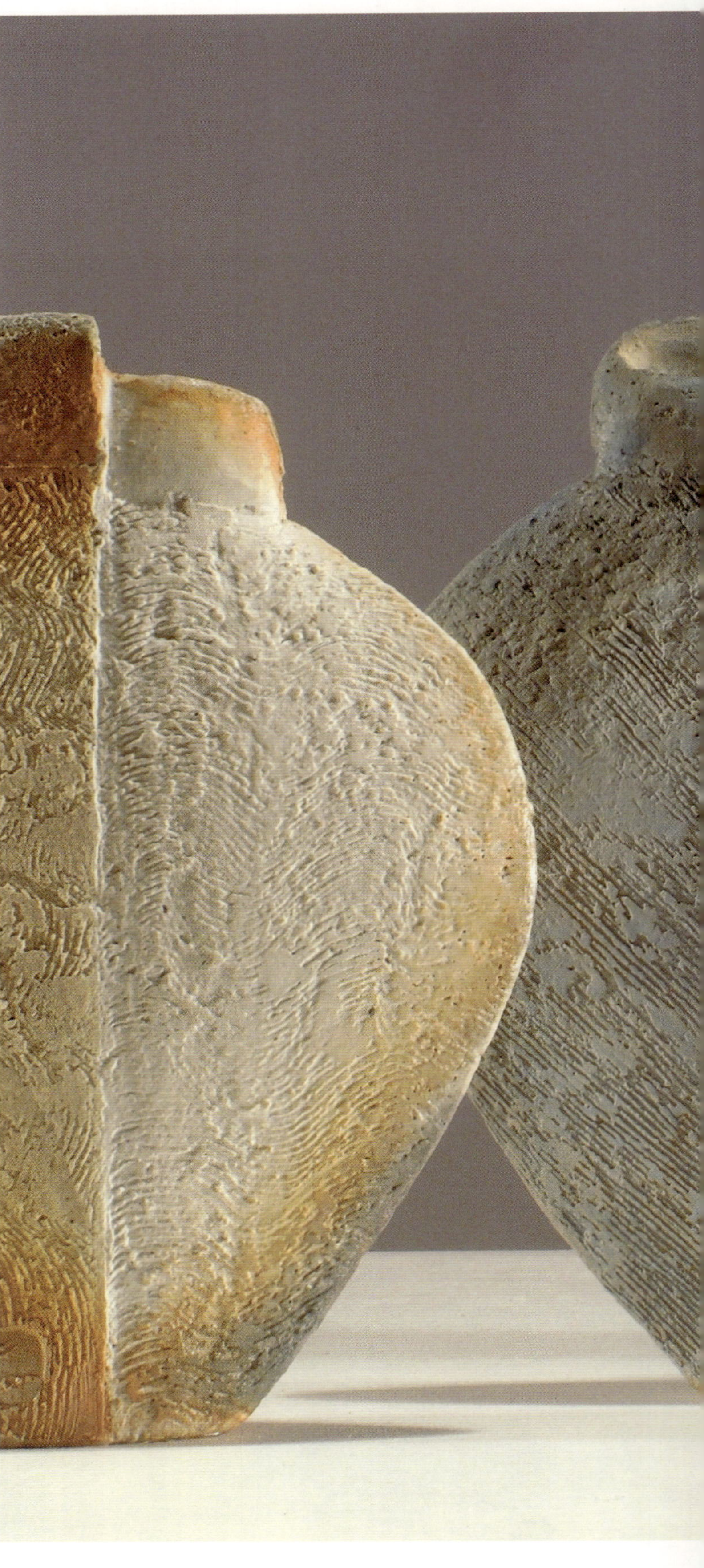

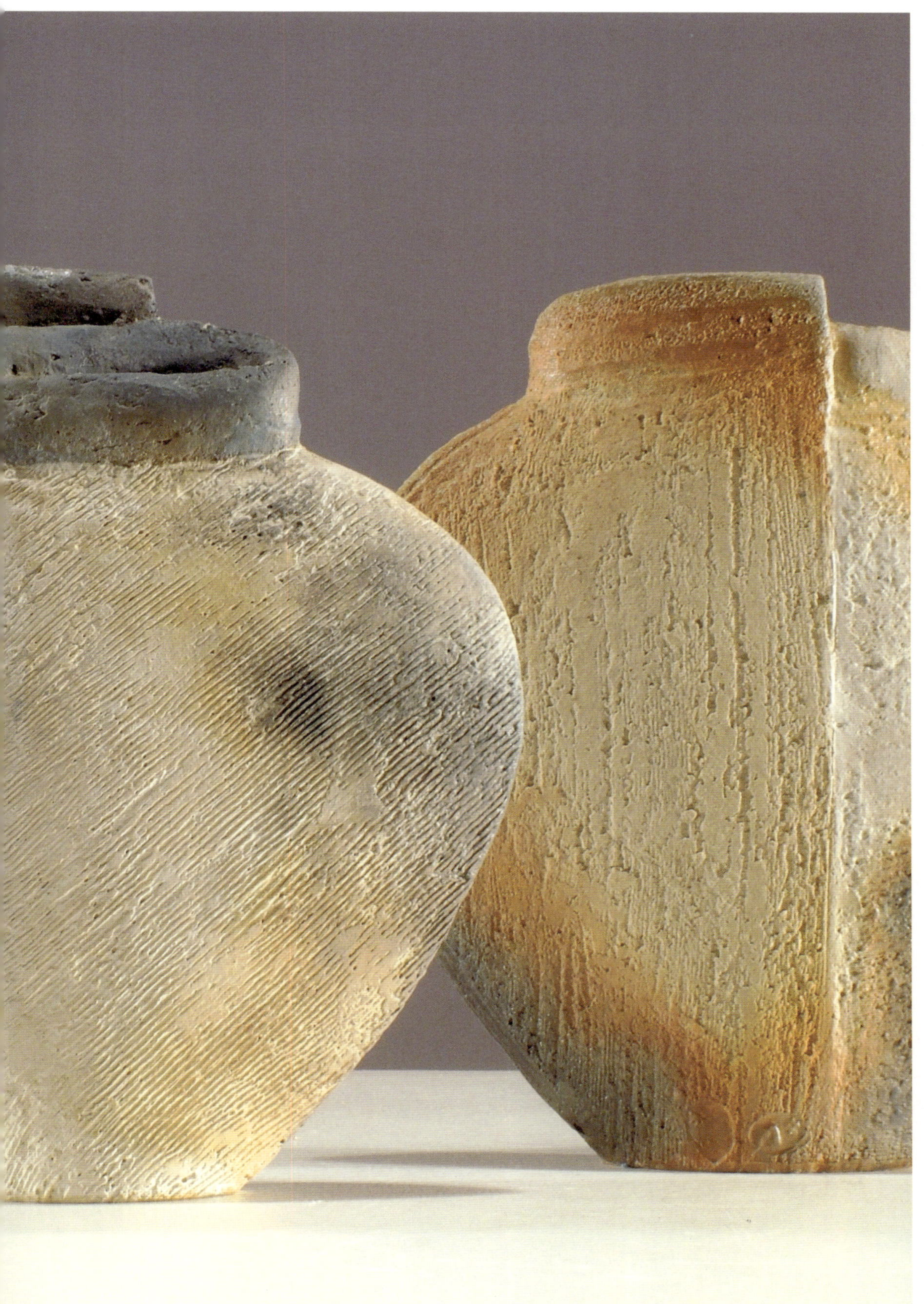

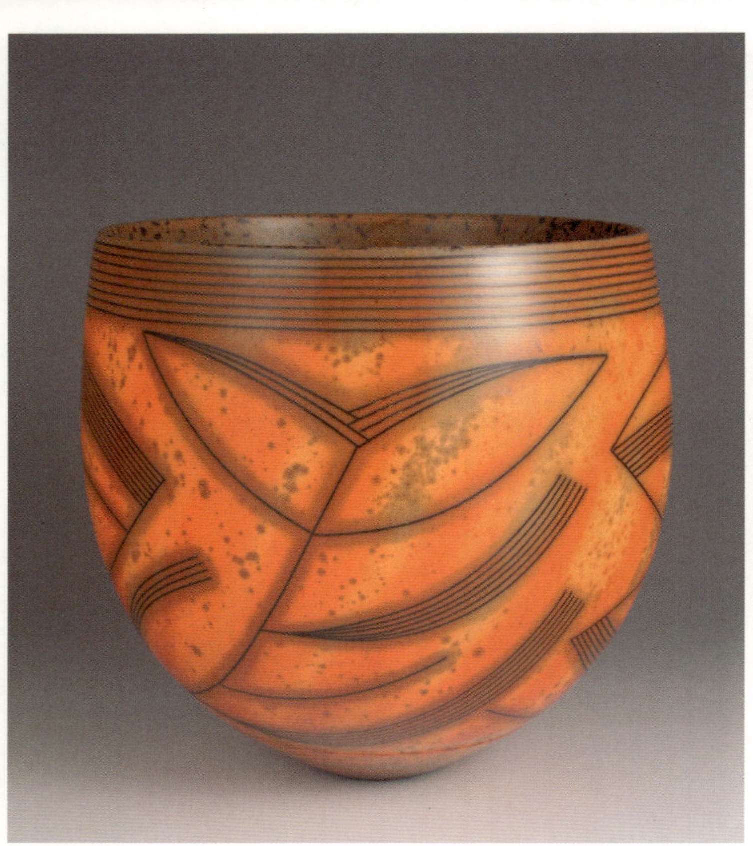

◁ DUNCAN ROSS
Terra Sigillata Bowl, 2007, H19cm
(Photo: Duncan Ross)

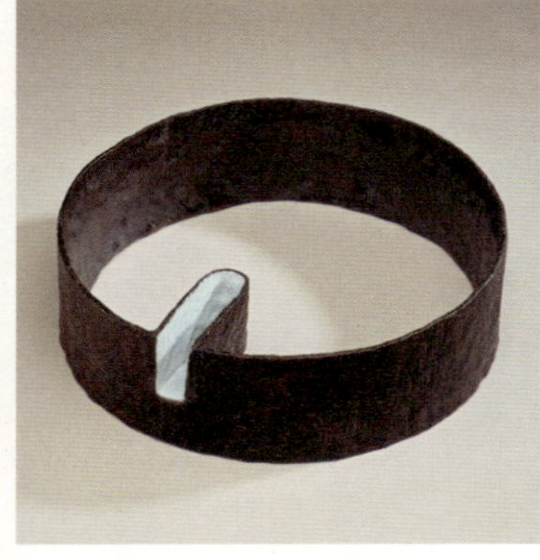

△ SUSAN DISLEY
Oxide Ring, pinched and coiled stoneware, 2006, Ø35cm approx.

▽ WALTER KEELER
Two Saltglaze Teapots, 2005, H14cm

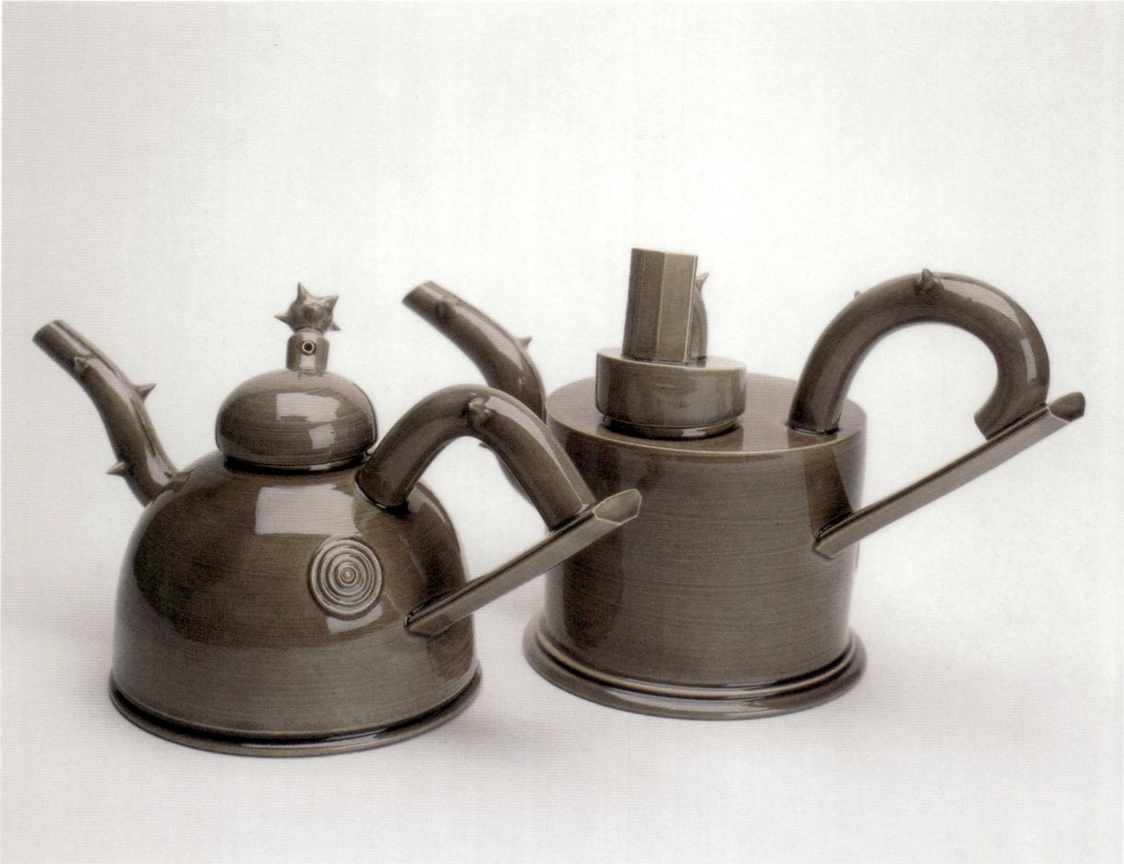

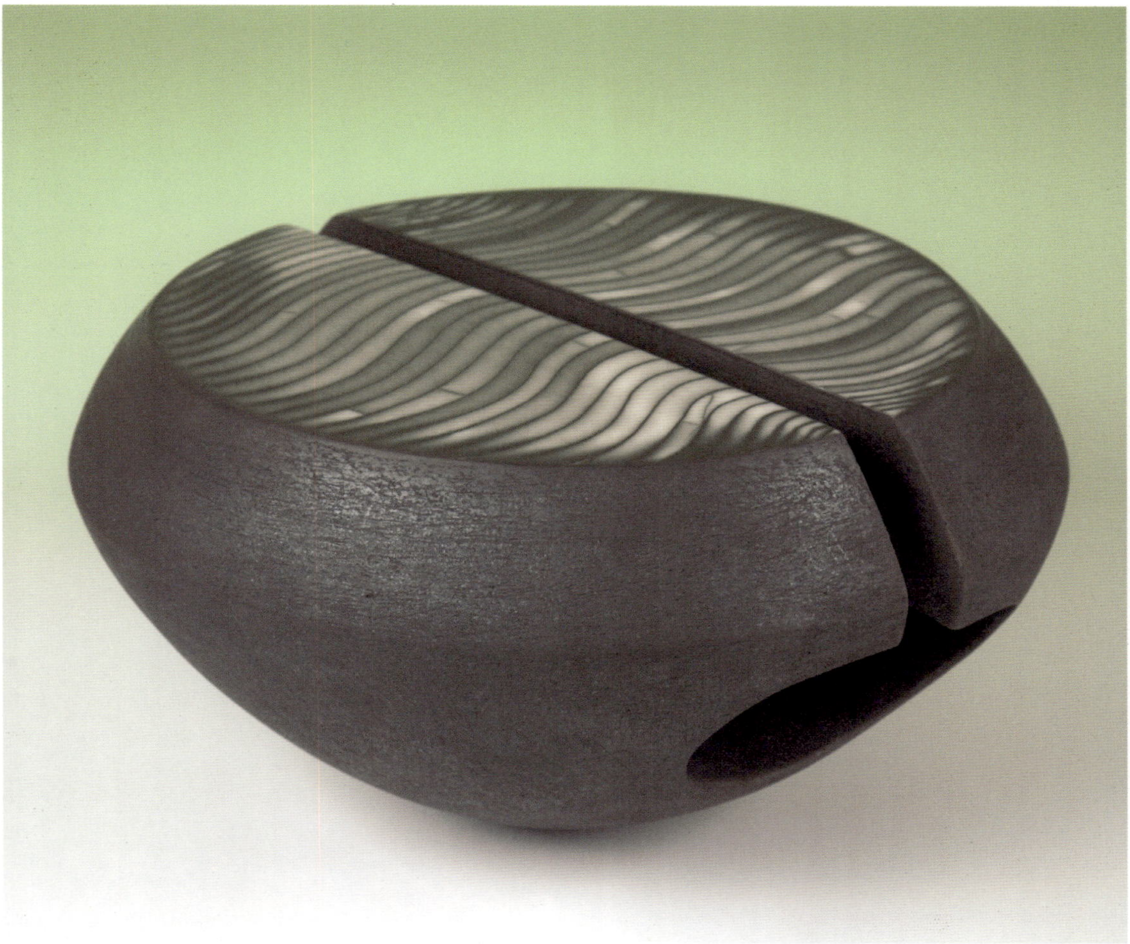

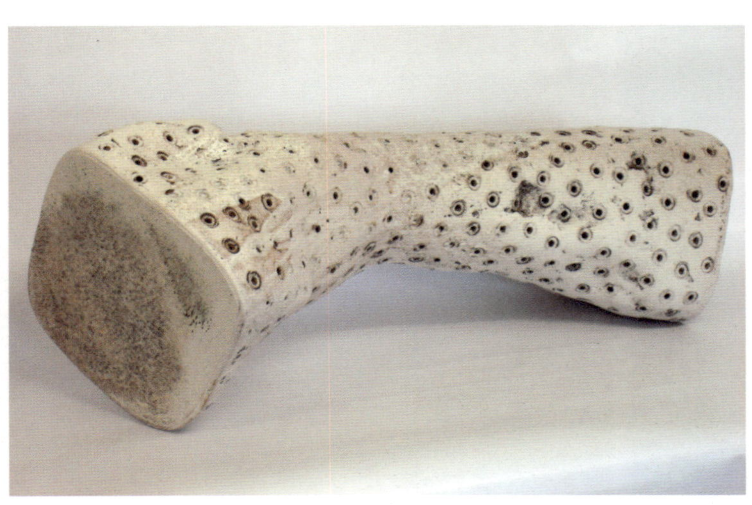

△ ASHRAF HANNA
Sculptural Form, raku, 2006, Ø40cm

◁ ANDRÉ HESS
Mitochondrium, crank clay, slips, oxides, 2007, L72cm

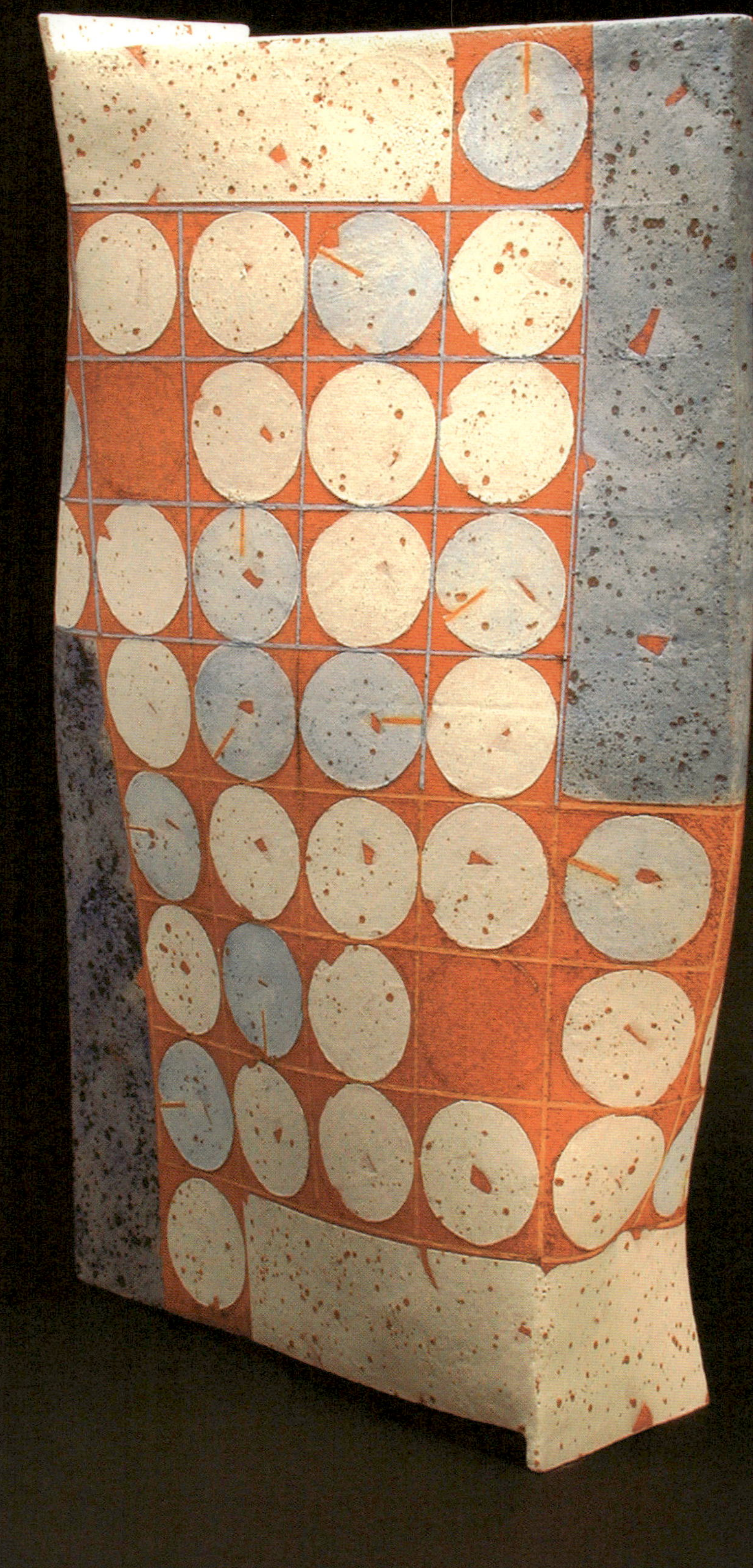

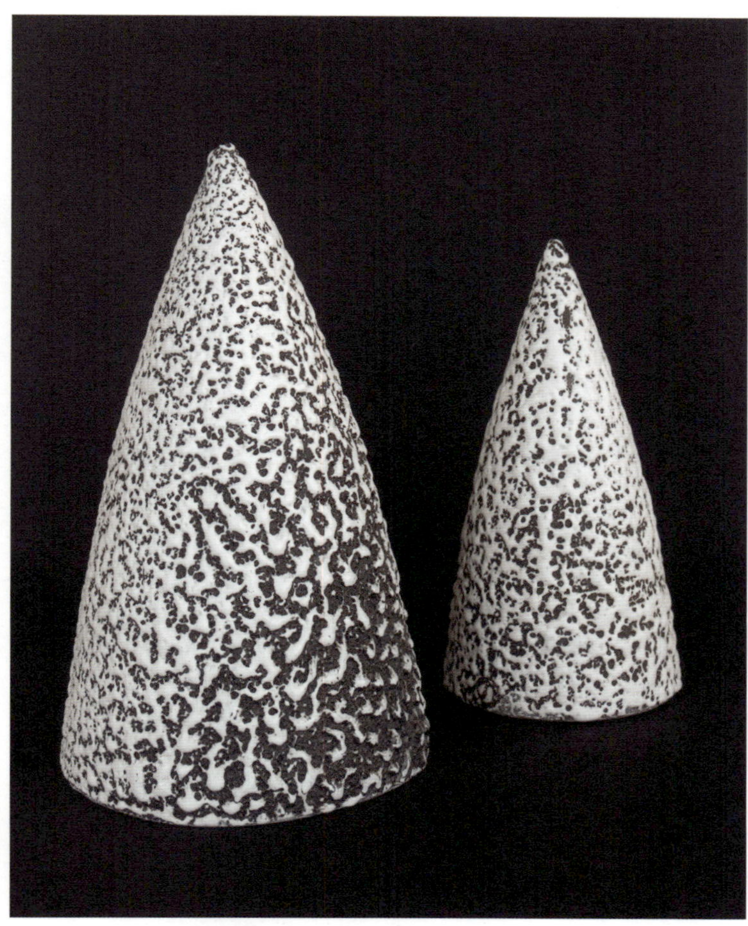

◁ EMMANUEL COOPER
City 1, City 2, stoneware, volcanic glaze, 2007, H70cm max

▽ GABRIELE KOCH
Large Sphere, porcelaneous T material, 2006, Ø52cm

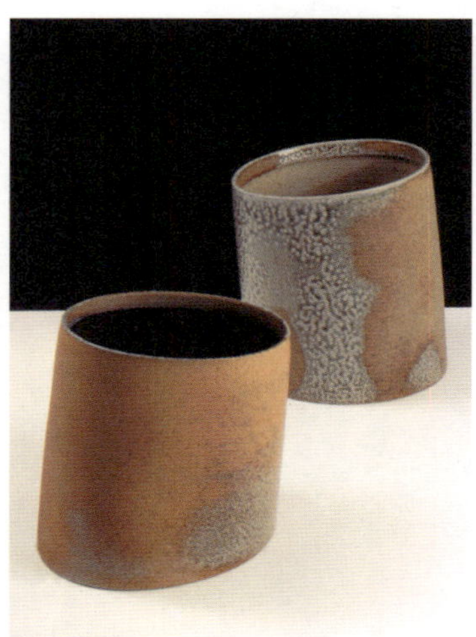

△ JANE HAMLYN
Erosion Duo, from *Empty Vessels* series, salt-glazed stoneware, 2005, H25cm max

◁ REGINA HEINZ
Time Zone, ceramic sculpture, 2006, H60cm

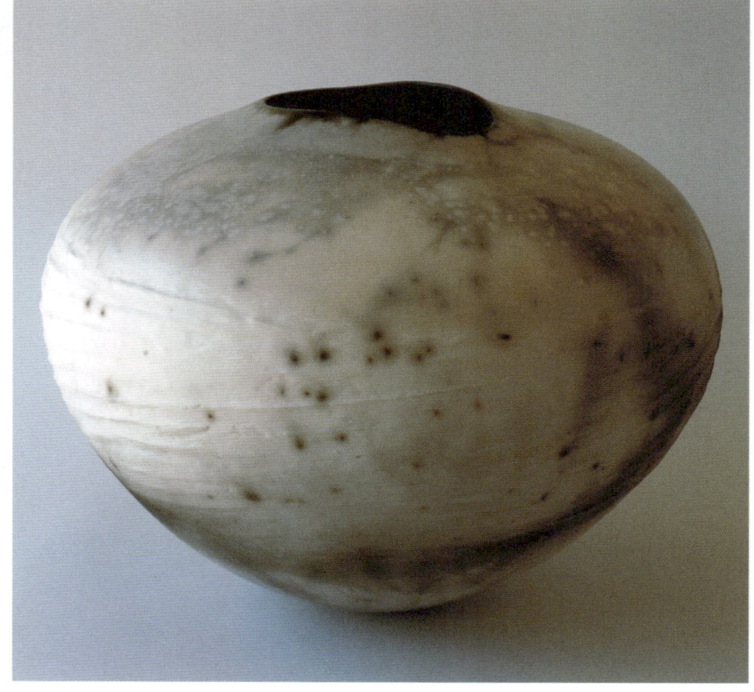

▽ AKI MORIUCHI
Moon Catcher, stoneware with porcelain inlay, 2006, L64cm

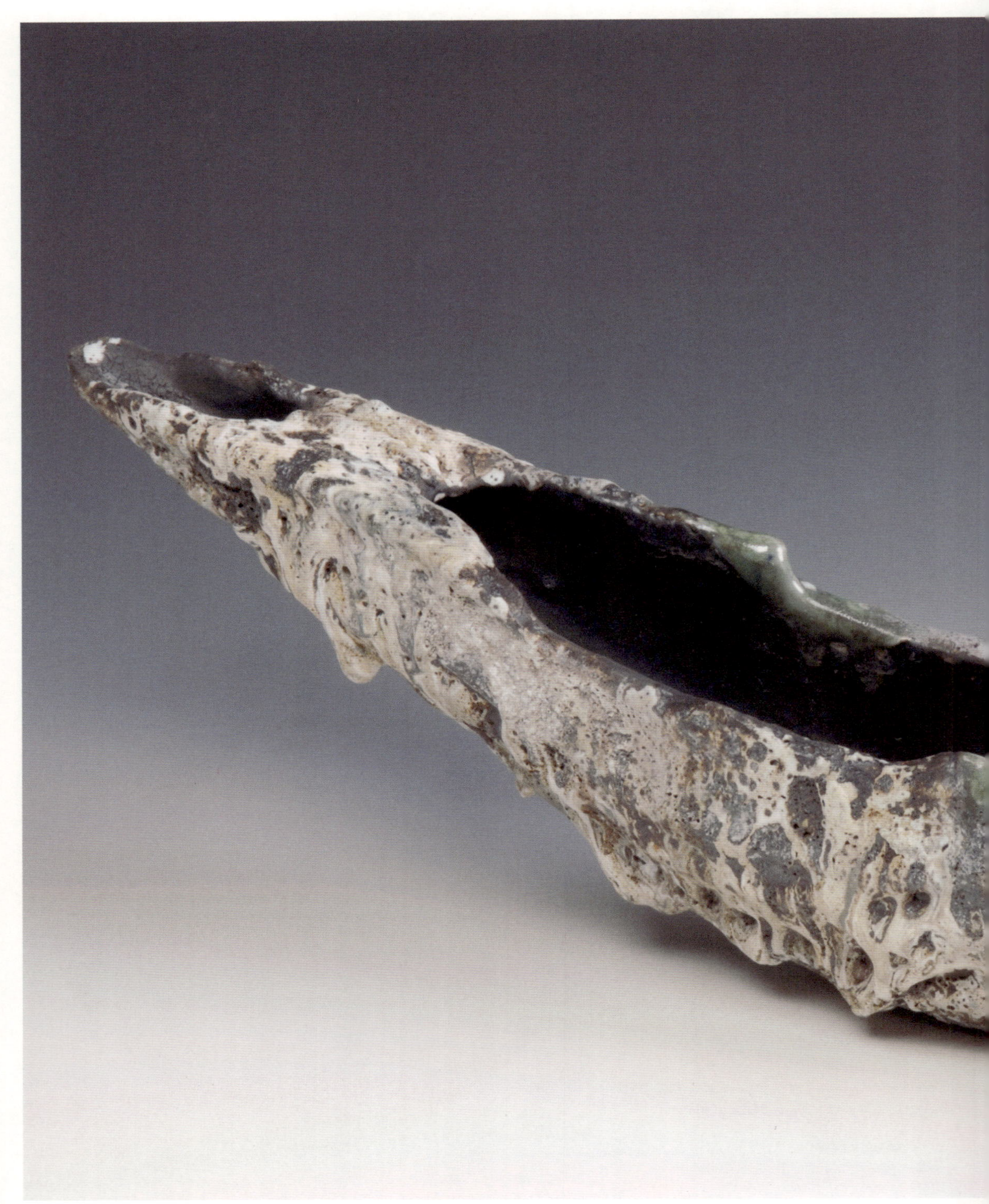

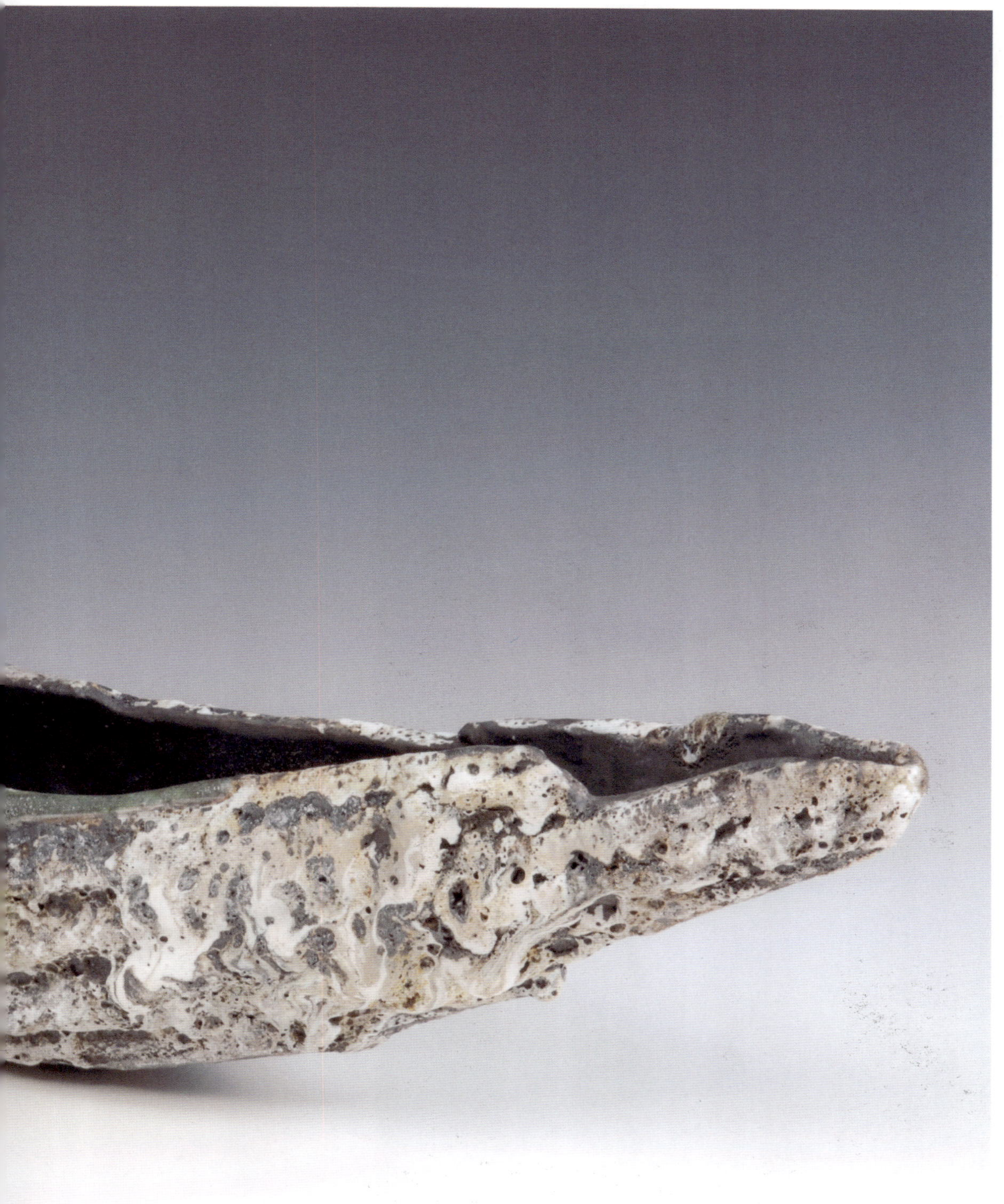

▷ TAKESHI YASUDA
Platter, porcelain, Ø40cm approx

▽ DAVID ROBERTS
Counterpoint Vessel, coil-built and raku-fired ceramic, 2007, H35cm

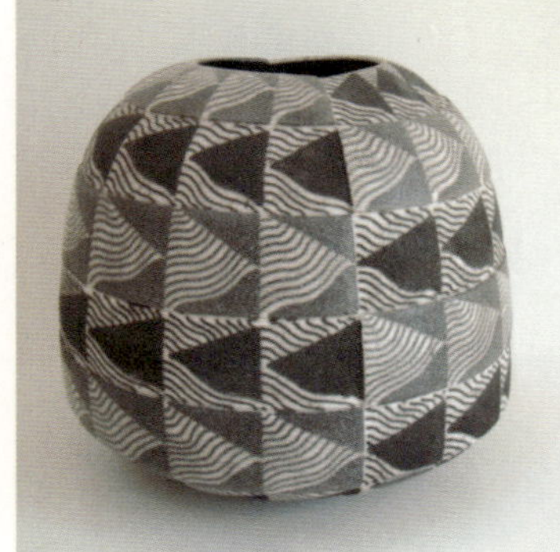

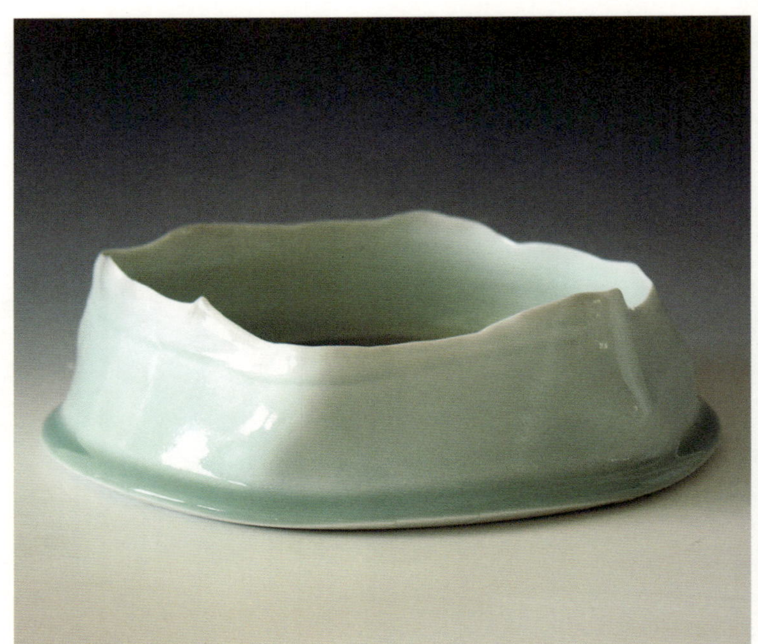

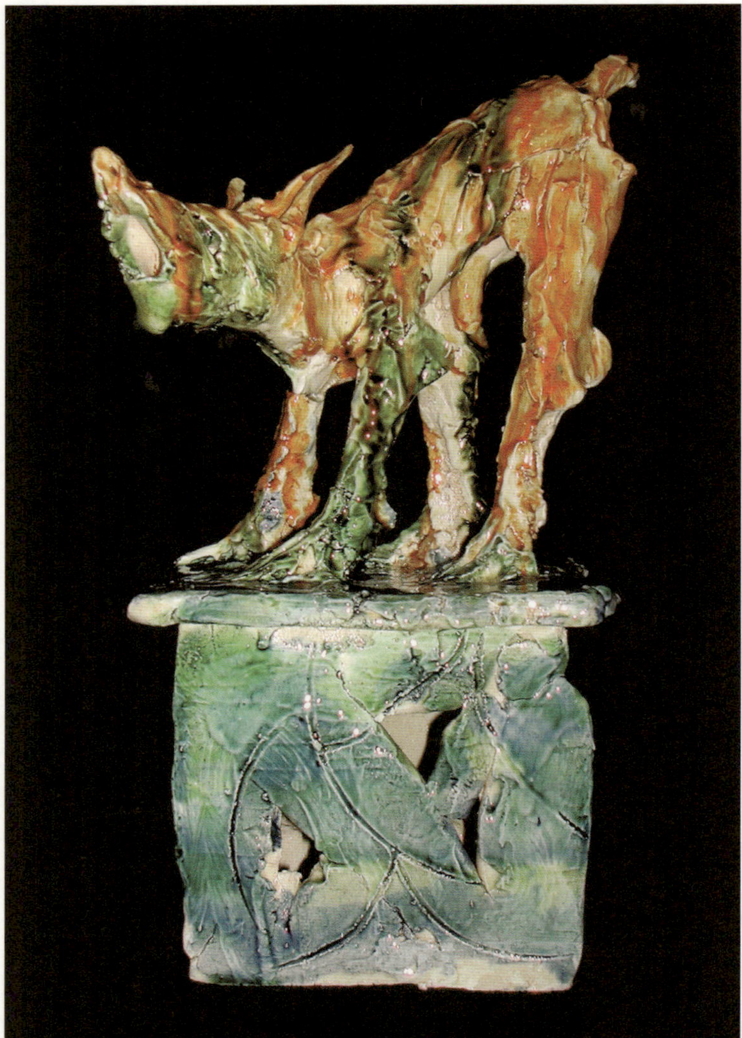

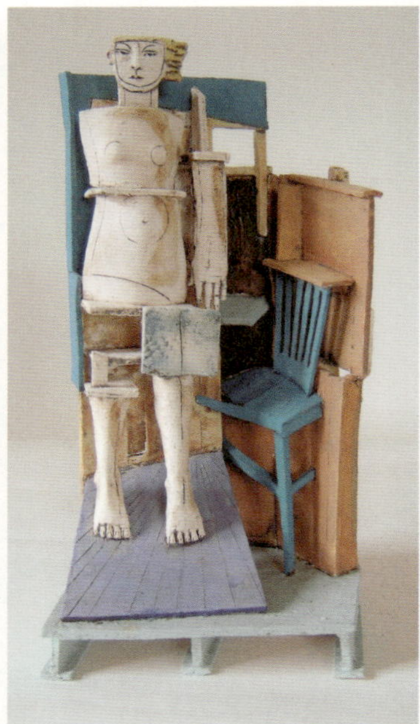

△ CHRISTY KEENEY
Figure with Chair, St Thomas and flax clay mix, 2007, H38cm

◁ IAN GREGORY
Howling Dog, high-fired earthenware, multiple glazes, H61cm

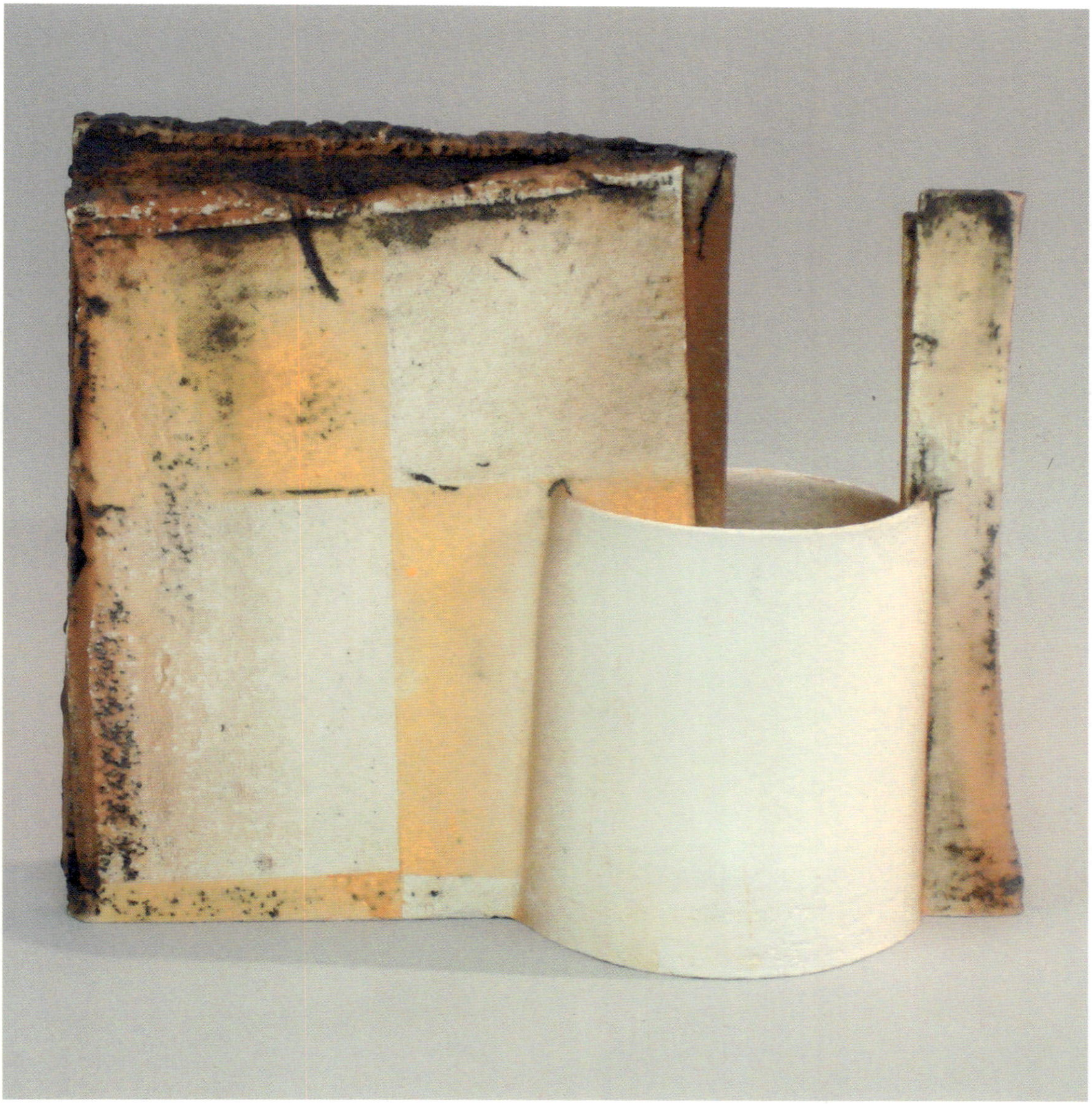

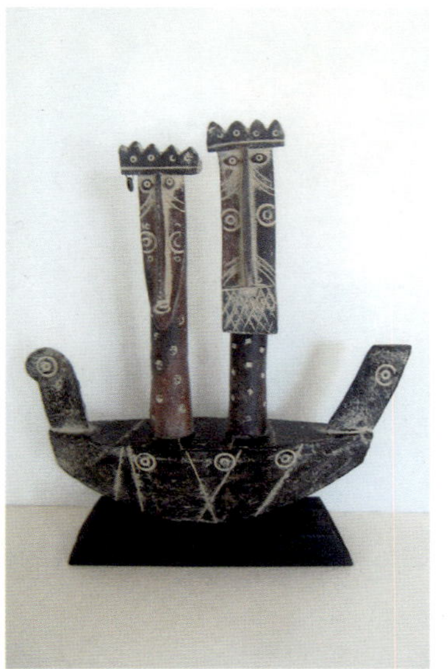

△ JOHN HIGGINS
Untitled, slabbed and thrown, slips, oxides, body stains and underglaze colours, 2007, H15cm

◁ JOHN MALTBY
Royal Barge, stoneware, 2007, H30cm

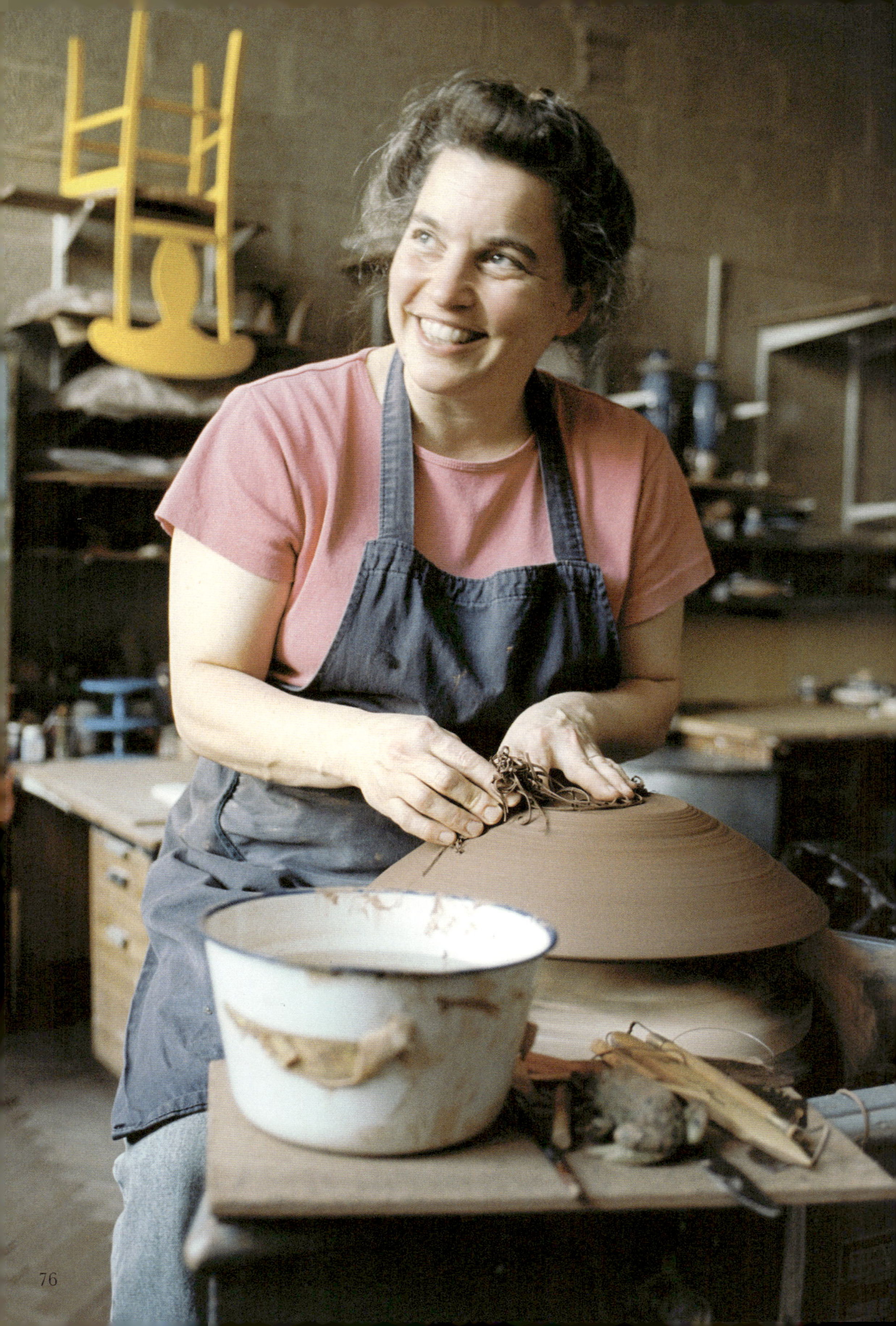

◁ Portrait of Morgen Hall
(Photo: Jan Baldwin)

CONTACT DETAILS

FELICITY AYLIEFF
Garden Flat, 14 Grosvenor Place, Bath BA1 6AX
Tel 01225 334136 (Home) or 01225 313492 (Studio)
Mob 07714 212124
Email aylieff@btinternet.com or felicity.aylieff@rca.ac.uk

PETER BEARD
Tanners Cottage, Welsh Road, Cubbington, Leamington Spa, Warwickshire CV32 7UB
Tel 029 2642 8481
Email peter@peterbeard.co.uk
Web www.peterbeard.co.uk

BEVERLY BELL-HUGHES
Dirion Conwy Road, Llandudno Junction, Conwy LL31 9AY
Tel 01492 572575

TERRY BELL-HUGHES
Dirion Conwy Road, Llandudno Junction, Conwy LL31 9AY
Tel 01492 572575

CLIVE BOWEN
Shebbear Pottery, Shebbear, Beaworthy, Devon EX21 5QZ
Tel 01409 281271
Email rosiebowen@talktalk.net

SANDY BROWN
3 Marine Parade, Appledore, Bideford, Devon EX39 1PJ
Tel 01237 478219
Email sandy@sandybrown.freeserve.co.uk
Web www.sandybrownarts.com

SIMON CARROLL
4C St Merryn Airfield, Padstow, Cornwall PL28 8PU
Tel 01841 520072
Email simonpcarroll@hotmail.com
Web www.simoncarroll.co.uk

NIC COLLINS
The Barn Pottery, North Bovey Road, Moretonhampstead, Devon TQ13 8PQ
Tel 01647 441198
Email nic.collins4@btopenworld.com
Web www.nic-collins.co.uk

EMMANUEL COOPER
Fonthill Pottery, 38 Chalcot Road, London NW1 8LP
Tel 020 7722 9090
Email emmanuelcooper@lineone.net

SUSAN DISLEY
Studio 3, Tan Gallop, Welbeck, Worksop North Nottinghamshire S80 3LW
Tel 01909 488989
Email info@susandisley.co.uk
Web www.susandisley.co.uk

MIKE DODD
The Pottery, Dove Workshops, Barton Road, Butleigh, Glastonbury, Somerset BA6 8TL
Tel/Fax 01458 850385

JACK DOHERTY
Hooks Cottage, Lea Bailey, Ross-on-Wye, Herefordshire HR9 5TY
Tel 01989 750644
Mob 07766 334917
Email jack.doherty@virgin.net
Web www.dohertyporcelain.com

DAVID FRITH
Brookhouse Pottery, Brookhouse Lane, Denbigh, Denbighshire LL16 4RE
Tel/Fax 01745 812805
Email frith@brookhousepottery.co.uk
Web www.brookhousepottery.co.uk

MARGARET FRITH
Brookhouse Pottery, Brookhouse Lane, Denbigh, Denbighshire LL16 4RE
Tel/Fax 01745 812805
Email frith@brookhousepottery.co.uk
Web www.brookhousepottery.co.uk

IAN GREGORY
The Studio, Crumble Cottage, Ansty, Dorchester, Dorset DT2 7PN
Tel/Fax 01258 880 891
Email igreg891@aol.com or ian@ian-gregory.co.uk
Web www.ian-gregory.co.uk

MORGEN HALL
Chapter Arts Centre, Market Road,
Canton, Cardiff CF5 1QE
Tel 029 2023 8716 or 029 2031 1050
ext 219
Email morgen@morgenhall.co.uk
Web www.morgenhall.co.uk

JANE HAMLYN
Millfield Pottery, Everton,
Doncaster DN10 5DD
Tel 01777 817723
Email janehamlyn@saltglaze.fsnet.co.uk

LISA HAMMOND
Maze Hill Pottery, The Old Ticket
Office, Woodlands Park Road,
Greenwich, London SE10 9XE
Tel/Fax 020 8293 0048
Email mazehill.pottery@virgin.net
Website www.mazehill-pottery.com

ASHRAF HANNA
Pen-Y-Daith,Chapel Lane, Keeston ,
Haverfordwest , Pembrokeshire SA62 6EH
Tel 01437 710774
Mob 07957 647990
Email ashrafhanna.ceramics@
btinternet.com
Web www.studiopottery.co.uk

REGINA HEINZ
52 Culmstock Road, London SW11 6LU
Tel/Fax 020 7738 0813
Mobile 07779 167229
Email regina_heinz@ceramart.net
Web www.ceramart.net

ANDRÉ HESS
32 Seaman Close, Park Street, St Albans,
Hertfordshire AL2 2NX
Tel/Fax 01727 874299
Email andrehess@
earthwaterfire.demon.co.uk

JOHN HIGGINS
32 Seaman Close, Park Street, St Albans,
Hertfordshire AL2 2NX
Tel/Fax 01727 874299
Email johnceramics@aol.com

JOANNA HOWELLS
2 Cwrt Isaf, Bridgend, Tythegston,
Mid-Glamorgan CF32 0ND
Tel 01656 784021
Email studio@joannahowells.co.uk
Web www.joannahowells.co.uk

LISA KATZENSTEIN
67 Tyrwhitt Road, London SE4 1QE
Tel/Fax 020 8694 2428
Email lisa@katzenstein.fslife.co.uk
Web www.lisakatzenstein.co.uk

WALTER KEELER
Moorcroft Cottage, Penallt,
Monmouth, Gwent NP25 4AH
Tel 01600 713 946
Fax 01600 712 530

CHRIS KEENAN
31 Balin House, Long Lane,
London SE1 1YQ
Tel 020 7701 2940
Fax 020 7403 1067
Email powellkeenan@compuserve.com
Web www.chriskeenan.com

CHRISTY KEENEY
Doonglebe, Newmills, Letterkenny,
Co. Donegal, Ireland.
Tel +353 (0)74 9167258
Email christykeeney@eircom.net
Web www.christykeeney.com

GABRIELE KOCH
147 Archway Road, London N6 5BL
Tel/Fax 020 8292 3169
Email gabrielekoch@blueyonder.co.uk

MARTIN LUNGLEY
67 Durham Road, Gateshead,
Tyne and Wear NE8 4AP
Mob 07811 038116
Email martinlungley@yahoo.com
Web studiopottery.co.uk

SOPHIE MacCARTHY
The Chocolate Factory, Farleigh Place,
Hackney, London N16 7SX
Tel 020 7690 5091
Email sophie_macc@yahoo.co.uk

JIM MALONE
Dairy Lea Cottage, Lessonhall, Wigton
Cumbria CA7 0EA
Tel 016973 45241

JOHN MALTBY
The Orchard House, Stoneshill,
Crediton, Devon EX17 4EF
Tel 01363 772753

GARETH MASON
7 Old Acre Road, Alton,
Hampshire, GU34 1NR
Tel 01420 543573
Email gi.mason@virgin.net

MARTIN McWILLIAM
Auf dem Koetjen 1, D-26209
Sandhatten, Germany
Tel +49 (0) 4482 8372
Email ceramics@martin-mcwilliam.de
Web www.martin-mcwilliam.de

DAVID MILLER
Rue du Ranc, 30190 Collorgues, France
Tel +33 (0) 466 819119
Email ceramicdavidmiller@yahoo.fr

AKI MORIUCHI
4 Menhyr Drive, Carbis Bay, St Ives,
Cornwall TR26 2QR
Tel 01736 793064
Email akimoriuchi@hotmail.com

JANE PERRYMAN
Wash Cottage, Clare Road, Hundon
Suffolk CO10 8DH
Tel 01440 786228
Email jane.perryman@btinternet.com
Web www.janeperryman.com

DAVID ROBERTS
England – Cressfield House, 44
Upperthong Lane, Holmfirth,
Huddersfield, Yorkshire HD9 3BQ
Tel 01484 685110
Italy – 14 Via Castello, Castello dc
Comano, 54015 Comano, MS, Italy.
Mob +44 (0) 7985 021 111
Email davidroberts@clara.net
Web www.davidroberts-ceramics.com

▽ Portrait of Takeshi Yasuda

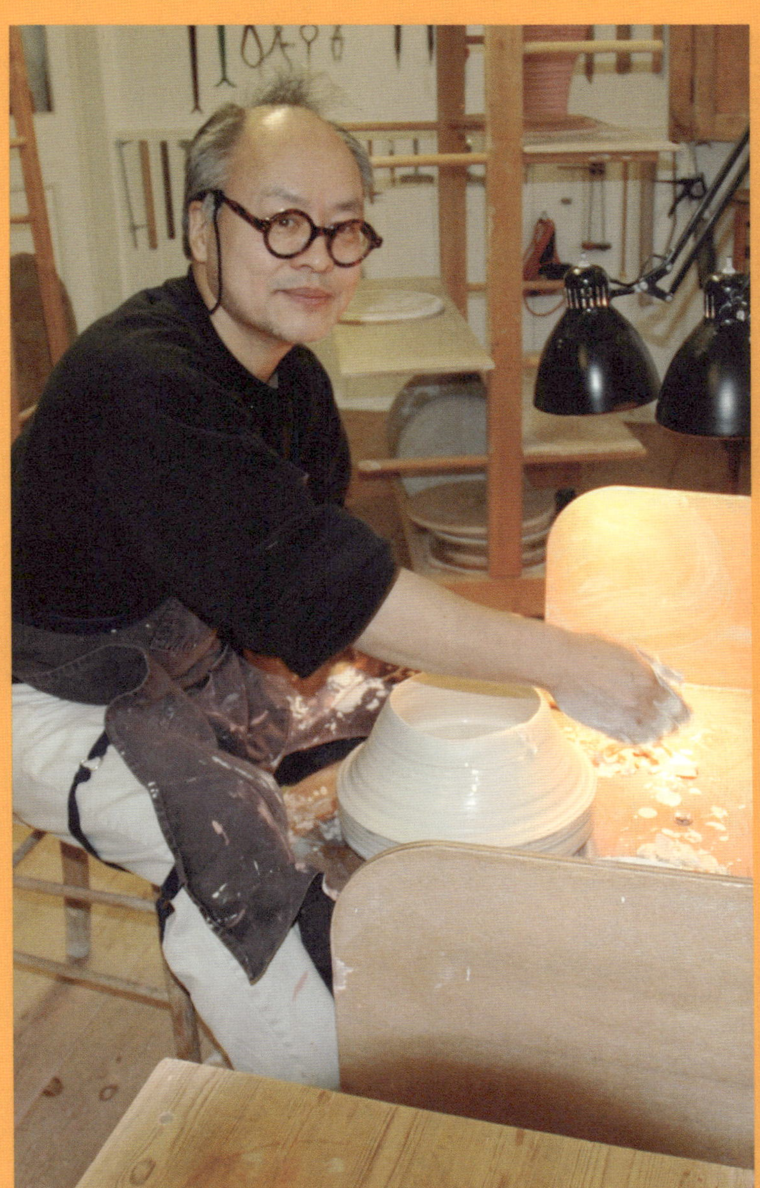

PHIL ROGERS
Lower Cefnfaes, Rhayader,
Powys LD6 5LT
Tel 01597 810875
Email phil@marstonpottery.wanadoo.co.uk
Web www.philrogerspottery.com

DUNCAN ROSS
Daneshay House, 69A Alma Lane,
Upper Hale, Farnham, Surrey GU9 0LT
Tel 01252 710704
Email duncanross.ceramics@virgin.net
Web www.duncanrossceramics.co.uk

ANTONIA SALMON
20 Adelaide Road, Nether Edge,
Sheffield S7 1SQ
Tel 0114 258 5971
Email antoniasalmon@blueyonder.co.uk
Web www.antoniasalmon-ceramics.co.uk

MICKI SCHLOESSINGK
Bridge Pottery, Cheriton, nr. Llanmadoc,
Gower, Swansea SA3 1BY
Tel 01792 386499
Email micki@mickisaltglaze.co.uk
Web www.mickisaltglaze.co.uk

JEREMY STEWARD
Wobage Farm Craft Workshops, Upton
Bishop, Ross-on-Wye, Herefordshire
HR9 7QP
Tel 01989 780448
Fax 01989 780495
Email info@workshops-at-wobage.co.uk
or jemsteward@btinternet.com

RUTHANNE TUDBALL
Temple Barn Pottery, Solomon's Temple,
Welborne, Dereham, Norfolk NR20 3LD
Tel 01362 858770
Web www.ruthannetudball.com

TINA VLASSOPULOS
29 Canfield Gardens, London NW6 3JP
Tel 020 7624 4582
Email tina@tinavlassopulos.com
Web www.tinavlassopulos.com

SARAH WALTON
Keepers, Bo-peep Lane, Alciston, Nr
Polegate, East Sussex BN26 6UH
Tel/Fax 01323 811517
Email sarah.walton@freenet.co.uk
Web www.sarahwalton.co.uk

TAKESHI YASUDA
Garden Flat, 14 Grosvenor Place,
Bath BA1 6AX
Tel 01225 334136 (Home) or
01225 313492 (Studio)
Mob 07815 068146
Email t.yasuda@btinternet.com

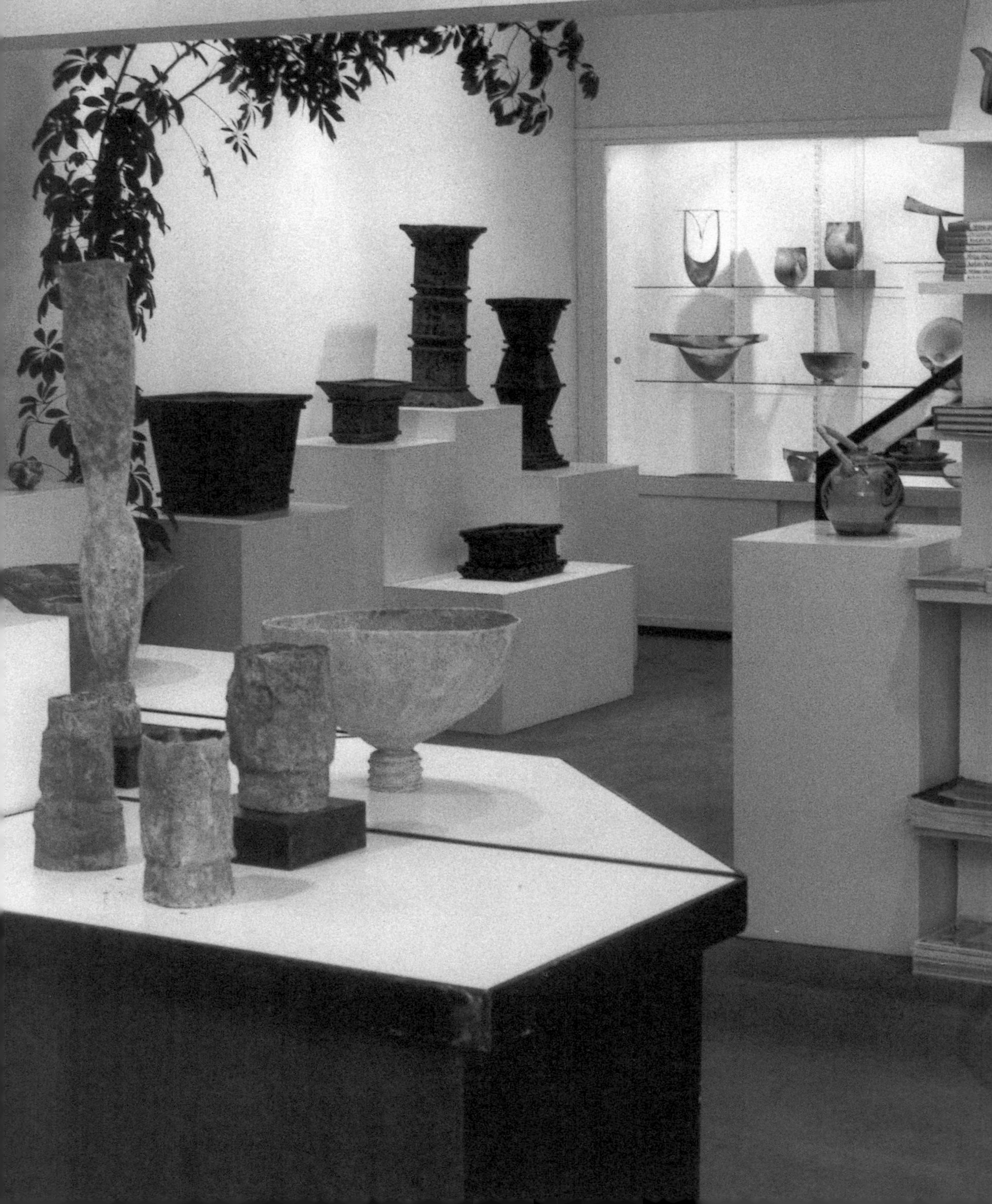
NEW MEMBERS SHOW

◁ New Members Show, 1990

CPA EXHIBITIONS 1960-2007

No full list of exhibitions arranged by the CPA of members work has been kept. The following lists have been compiled as fully as possible from existing records. Apologies for anyone omitted. The list is of exhibitions held in the Lowndes Court and Marshall Street shops in London.

Exhibitions at the Craftsmen Potters Shop, Lowndes Court, London W1

1960
- Ray Finch 'Stoneware' (May, June)
- Rosemary D. Wren 'Animals and Birds in Saltglaze' special solus (July)
- Murray Fieldhouse 'Stoneware' (August)

1961
- Eileen Lewenstein 'Stoneware' (February)
- Denis Moore and Michael Buckland (March)
- Audrey Blackman 'Stoneware and Earthenware Figures' (March)
- Associates Exhibition (July)
- John Dan 'Stoneware'
- Harry Horlock Stringer 'Earthenware'
- Helen Walters 'Saltglaze, Stoneware and Porcelain'
- Vera Tollow 'Stoneware' (November)

1962
- Teapot Exhibition (April)
- Stanislas Reychan 'Pottery Sculpture' (April)
- Holkham Studio Pottery (June)
- Tony Benham 'Pots' (June)
- Michael Skipwith 'Pots' (July)
- Peter Lane 'Pots' (August)
- Green Dene 'Pottery Pots' (August)
- Tessa and Annette Fuchs 'Pots' (September)
- Pauline Thompson 'Pots' (September)
- Brian Rochford 'Pots' (September)
- Alan Wallwork 'Pots' (September, October)
- Lavender Groves 'Pots' (October)
- French Pots and Textiles (November)
- David Eeles 'Pots' (November)
- Christmas Display (November, December)

1963
- Eric Stockl 'Pots' (February)
- Maria Seviers 'Pots' (February)
- Jeremy Harper 'Pots' (March)
- Paul and Yvette Brown 'Pots' (March)
- Louis Hanssen 'Pots' (May)
- All members 'Casseroles' (June)
- John Solly 'Pots' (June)
- Tom Plowman 'Pots' (September)
- Barbara Cass 'Pots' (September)
- Tessa and Annette Fuchs (September)
- Colin Pearson 'Pots' (September, October)
- Laurence Keen 'Pots' (October)
- Trevor Logan 'Pots' (October)
- Denis Moore and Michael Buckland 'Stoneware' (October)
- Tony Benham 'Pots' (October)
- Bryan Newman and Raymond Silverman (November)

1964
- John Berry 'Pots' (March, April)
- Full Members 'Pots for Plants' (May, June)
- Rosemary D. Wren 'Saltglaze and Stoneware' special solus (June)
- Group Exhibition. Tony Benham, Keith Harding, Derek Davis, Bryan Rochford, Tessa Fuchs, Anne Thalmessinger, Annette Fuchs (October)
- Michael and Sheila Casson 'Stoneware' special solus (November)

1965
- Group Exhibition: Katharine Pleydell-Bouverie, Audrey Blackman, Paul Barren, Michael Buckland, Henry Hammond, Denis Moore (April, May)
- Joanna Constantinidis and Pamela Greenwood 'Pots' (May)
- Full Members 'Coffee Pots' (June)
- Canadian Guild of Potters 'Canadian Ceramics' (July)
- Fay Russell and Emmanuel Cooper 'Stoneware' (September)
- Trentham de Leliva 'Stoneware' (October)
- Barbara Cass 'Stoneware' special solus (October, November)
- George Rainer 'Stoneware' (November)

1966
- John Berry 'Ceramic Sculpture'
- Keith Harding 'Ceramics' (January)
- Full Members 'Storage Jars' (June)
- Geoffrey Whiting 'Stoneware and

Porcelain' (September, October)
- Eric Stockl 'Pots' (October)
- David Leach 'Stoneware and Porcelain' (November)

1967

- Craftsmen Potters Association of South Wales (May)
- Full Members 'Cooking Pots' (July)

Exhibitions at the Craftsmen Potters Shop, 7 Marshall Street, London W1

1968

- Five Potters: Katharine Pleydell-Bouverie, Joanna Constantinidis, Ray Finch, Rosemary D. Wren, Robin Welch (July)
- Harry Davis 'Pots' (July)
- George Rainer 'Pots' (October)
- Six Potters: Alan Wallwork, David Leach, Ian Auld, Colin Pearson, Bryan Newman, Michael Casson (November)

1969

- Open Sculpture Exhibition

1970

- Bernard Rooke 'Ceramics' (October, November)

1971

- Coxwold Pottery 'Stoneware and Wood Fired Earthenware' (September)
- Harry and May Davis 'Stoneware and Porcelain' (October)
- Bryan Newman 'Pots and Sculpture' (November)

1972

- South Wales Potters (April)
- Alan Caiger-Smith 'Earthenware' (May)
- Danny Killick 'Stoneware' (June)
- Wally Keeler, Mike Dodd, West Marshall 'Pots' (September)

1973

- Full Members 'Porcelain' (April)
- Tessa Fuchs 'Objects' (June)
- Danny Killick 'Stoneware' (July, August)
- Alan Caiger-Smith and Colleagues from Aldermaston (October)
- Bryan Newman 'Pots and Sculpture' (November)
- Michael Casson

1974

- Full Members 'Ceramic Boxes' (March)
- Mary Rogers, Mary Rich, John Maltby 'Ceramics' (June)
- David Lloyd Jones and Scott Marshall 'Pots' (September)

1975

- Full members 'Candlesticks and Candleholders' (February)
- Michael Cardew and Associates 'Recent Pots' (April)
- Russell Collins and Terry Bell-Hughes 'Recent Work' (October, November)

1976

- New Members: Val Barry, Dave Edmonds, Dorothy Feibleman, Ian Gregory, Peter Phillips, Andrew Richardson, Geoffrey Swindell (February)
- Six Potters: Paul Barron, Audrey Blackman, Katharine Pleydell-Bouverie, Michael Buckland, Henry Hammond, Denis Moore (April, May)
- Full Members 'A Souvenir of Britain' (May)
- Deirdre Burnett, Sheila Casson, Janice Tchalenko 'Recent Work' (July)
- Joanna Constantinidis 'Recent Work' (September)
- Emmanuel Cooper, Derek Davis, Eileen Lewenstein 'Recent Work' (November)

1977

- New Members: Peter Beard, Margery Clinton, Tina Forester, John Lomas, Christine Anne Richards (February)
- Clive Davis, Andrew Holden, Siddig El'Nigoumi (May)
- Peter Dick 'Recent Work' (September)

1978

- New Members: Michael Bayley, Margaret Berkowitz, Ray Gardiner, Jane Hamlyn, Gary Standige, Sarah Walton, Andrew and Joanna Young (February)
- Modern German Ceramics (March)
- Delan Cookson, Geoffrey Eastop, Geoffrey Swindell 'Recent Work' (June)
- Full Members 'Teapots' (September)
- John Davies, Peter Starkey, Derek Emms, David Winkley 'New Work' (November)

1979

- New Members: Mick Arnup, Ruth and Alan Barrett-Danes, Bill Brown, Dartington Pottery Training Workshop, John Jelfs, William Mehornay, John Pollex, Peter Simpson (February)
- Eric Mellon, Marianne de Trey, Ray Silverman, Mary White 'Recent Work' (March)
- Geoffrey Whiting 'New work' (July)
- Ray Finch 'Recent Work' (September)
- Full Members 'Bowls' (November)

1980

- New Members: Mick Arnup, Ruth Franklin, Ewen Henderson, Alan Heaps, Mal Magson, David Morris, Peter Smith, Nigel Wood (February)
- Nick Homoky, Gordon Baldwin, Ruth and Alan Barrett-Danes, Peter Simpson 'New Work' (March)
- Full Members 'Jugs' (May)
- David Lloyd Jones 'Recent Work' (June)
- David Leach 'Stoneware and Porcelain' (September)
- Full Members 'Porcelain' (October)
- Jane Hamlyn, Jim Malone, Gary Standige 'New Work' (November)

1981

- New Members: Chris Ashton, Suzi Cree, Micky Doherty, David Frith, Neil Ions, Ruth King, Andrew McGarva, Dave Roberts, Jim Robison, Warren and Deborah Storch, Byron Temple, John Ward (February)
- Val Barry, Peter Beard, Dorothy Feibleman, Peter Meanley 'Recent Work' (March)
- Full Members 'Pots for Plants and Flowers' (May)
- Terry Bell-Hughes, Dartington Pottery and Alan Pirie 'Recent Work' (July)
- Robin Welch 'Recent Work' (June)

- Colin Pearson 'New Work' (September)
- Peter Smith, Sarah Walton, Andrew and Joanna Young 'Recent Work' (October)

1982

- Full Members 'Potters Pots' (February)
- David Frith and John Maltby 'New Work' (March)
- Ruth Franklyn, Neil Ions, David Robert, John Ward 'Recent Work'
- Mary Rogers 'Stoneware and Porcelain' (July)
- Wally Keeler 'Saltglaze' (September)
- 'New French Ceramics' (October)
- John Leach and Svend Bayer 'New Work' (November)

1983

- New Members: Ian Byers, Miguel Espinosa, John Huggins, David Miller, Angela Verdon, Takeshi Yasuda (March)
- Janet Leach 'New Work' (April)
- Fifteen Full Members 'Decorated Porcelain' (June)
- 50 Potters 'Studio Ceramics' (September)
- Paul Barron, Henry Hammond, Siddig El'Nigoumi and Nigel Wood '4 from Farnham' (September)
- Ewen Henderson and Janice Tchalenko (October)
- Associates Exhibition

1984

- New Members: Clive Bowen, Daphne Carnegy, Richard Launder, Magdalene Odundo, David Scott, Sabina Teuteberg, Caroline Whyman (February)
- Graham Burr, Joanna Constantinidis, Ruth King, Magdalene Odundo, Geoffrey Swindell 'The Individual Eye' (April)
- 40 Members 'Especially for the Table: A new look at tableware' (June)
- Maggie Angus Berkowitz, Audrey Blackman, Barbara Colls, Tessa Fuchs, Alan Heaps, Neil Ions, Andrew McGarva, Eric James Mellon, Stanislas Reychan, Rosemary D. Wren, Peter Crotty 'People and Other Animals' (October)
- Alan Caiger-Smith and Aldermaston Pottery (November)

1985

- New Members: John Ablitt, John Dunn, John Gibson, Anthony Philips, Henry Pim, John Wheeldon (February)
- Margery Clinton, Peter Dick, Micky Doherty, David Miller and Dave Roberts 'Playing with Fire' (April)
- David Scott and Sabina Teuteberg 'New Work' (May)
- David Lloyd Jones and Takeshi Yasuda 'Stoneware and Porcelain' (June)
- Shades of Blue (August)
- John Glick 'Decorated Pots from the USA' (October)
- John Ward 'New Pots' (November)

1986

- Potters 86: An exhibition to celebrate the publication of the 7th edition of *Potters*, the illustrated directory of the work of the full members of the Craftsmen Potters Association of Great Britain (February)
- New Members: Sandy Brown, Russell Coates, Jack Doherty, Phil Rogers, Mary Wandrausch, Sasha Wardell (March)
- Tessa Fuchs, Rosemary D. Wren and Peter Crotty 'All Creatures Great and Small' (April)
- Jim Robinson and Peter Stoodley 'Pots for Landscape' (June)
- In the Pink: A Summer Exhibition (July)
- Jane Hamlyn 'Saltglaze' (September)
- John Maltby 'New Decorated Pots' (November)

1987

- David Roberts 'Selected Raku forms' (May)
- New Members: Jutka Fischer, Gilles Le Corre, James Tower, Josie Walter, Anna Lambert, Archie McCall, Tina Vlassopulos, Gary Warnell (May)
- Emmanuel Cooper 'New porcelain and glaze installation' (June)
- Alan Barrett-Danes, Audrey Blackman, Alan Heaps, Colin Kellam, Eric James Mellon, Mary Wandrausch 'The Human Touch' (July)
- Derek Clarkson, Mike Dodd, Derek Emms, Henry Hammond, David Leach, Janet Leach, John Leach, Jim Malone, Mary Rich, Phil Rogers, Marrianne de Trey, Geoffrey Whiting, Takeshi Yasuda 'The Leach Tradition: A creative force' (November)
- Colin Pearson 'New Pots' (December)

1988

- Paul Soldner 'Ceramic Forms' (January)
- Maggie Barnes, Sandy Brown, Gordon Cooke, Marian Gounce, Ann Harris, Peter Moss, Karl and Ursula Scheid, Louise Gilbert Scott, Geoffrey Swindell, Sutton Taylor 'Bottles and Bowls' (April)
- Michael Cardew, Seth Cardew, Ray Finch, Peter Dick, Clive Bowen, Svend Bayer, Ursula Mommens, Michael O'Brien 'Michael Cardew and Friends' (May)
- Jackie Brett, Margaret Poulstone, Susan Nemeth, Peter Tring, Simon Ward and Mary Cunningham Wilson 'The Batsford Craft Award 1988: Winners Exhibition' (July)
- Peter Beard 'New Ceramics' (September)
- David Frith 'New Work' (November)

1989

- Mike Dodd 'New Stoneware: Out of the Earth' (February)
- Dart Pottery 'New Work' (March)
- Come into the Garden (April)
- Takeshi Yasuda 'Stoneware' (May)
- Derek Emms, Derek Clarkson, David Leach, Eileen Lewenstein, Mary Rich 'Small is Beautiful'
- Ian Byers, David Cohen, Christine Constant, Jill Crowley, John Dunn, Dennis Farrell, Keiko Hasegawa, David Howard Jones, David Miller, Anna Noel, Sarah Noel, Tim Proud, David Roberts 'Raku Today' (July)
- Neil Ions, Anna Lambert, John Maltby, Rosemary D. Wren, Kate Byrne, Jennie Hale, Jeremy James, Laurel Keeley 'High Flyers: Birds in and on Ceramics' (August)
- Clive Bowen, Sandy Brown, Peter Dick, Jane Hamlyn, Phil Rogers, Josie Walter,

Mary Wandrausch, Andrew and Joanna Young 'Feast: Pots for Food' (September)
- Janet Leach 'New Work' (November)
- Teapots (November)

Showcases
Tessa Fuchs 'Animals in Clay' (April) / Jack Doherty 'Inlaid Porcelain' (May) / Sheila Casson 'Decorated Stoneware' (June) / John Gibson 'New Work' (July) / Barbara Colls 'Stoneware' (August) / John Wheeldon 'Lustres' (September) / Annette Fuchs 'Stoneware and Porcelain' (October) / Clive Davies 'Colourful Stoneware' (October) / Derek Clarkson 'Bottles and Bowls' (October)

1990
- Associate Members 'Clayworks' (February)
- John Maltby 'Recent Work' (April)
- New Members: Seth Cardew, Margaret Frith, Karin Hessenberg, Emily Myers, Duncan Ross, Antonia Salmon (May)
- Anna Lambert 'New Pots' (June)
- Colin Pearson, Martin Lewis, Russell Coates, Derek Clarkson, Deirdre Burnett, Terry Bell-Hughes, Peter Beard, Ruth Barrett-Danes, Peter Lane, Caroline Whyman, Jane Perryman, Helen Swain 'Light Fantastic: Porcelain Today' (July)
- Setting Out: Selected Work by Art School Graduates
- Ray Finch and Winchcombe Pottery 'Wood-fired Stoneware and Salt Glaze' (September)
- David Leach 'Sixty Years a Potter' (October)
- Michael Casson 'New Work' (November)
- Pots for Christmas (December)

Showcases
Eileen Lewenstein 'New Work' (February) / Susan Nemeth (March) / Mary Rich (April) / Emmanuel Cooper 'New Work' (May) / Dorothy Feibleman 'New Work' (June) / Alan Barrett-Danes (July) / David Lloyd Jones (August) / Carolyn Genders (September) / Micky Schloessingk (October) / John Pollex 'New Earthenware' (December)

1991
- Handle with Care: Pots by Members of the Northern Potters Association (February)
- Tina Vlassopulos (March)
- Geoffrey Fuller (April)
- New Members: Tim Andrews, Loretta Braganza, Carlo Briscoe, John Calver, Roger Cockram, Edward Dunn, Christopher Green, Nigel Lambert, Richard Phethean, Mick Pinner, Patrick Sargent, Ruthanne Tudball, Gary Wood (May)
- Daphne Carnegy 'Maiolica' (June)
- Antonia Salmon 'Burnished Earthenware' (July)
- Setting Out '91: Selected work by Art School Graduates (August)
- Phil Rogers 'Woodfired Stoneware and Porcelain' (October)
- Sandy Brown 'Ritual Objects' (October)
- John Pollex 'New Earthenware' (November)

Showcases
Ruth King (March) / Peter Starkey (April) / Mick Pinner 'Garden Pots' (May) / Owen Thorpe 'Stoneware' (June) / Beverly Bell-Hughes / Alan Wallwork (August) / Mal Magson 'New Work' (September) / Ruthanne Tudball 'Saltglaze' (October) / Geoffrey Eastop 'Pots Past and Present' (November)

1992
- Fireworks: Ceramics by recently elected Professional Members (February)
- Svend Bayer 'Wood-fired Pots' (March)
- Sabina Teuteberg (April)
- Homage to Catalona: Ceramics from Potters in Catalonia (May)
- Patrick Sargent 'Touch of the Fire' (June)
- Tessa Wolf Murray (June)
- Felicity Aylieff, Gordon Baldwin, John Colbeck, Ewen Henderson, Gabriele Koch, Magdalene Odundo, Takeshi Yasuda 'Poetics of Fire' (July)
- Setting Out: Selected work by Art School Graduates (August)
- Liz Gale (August)
- David Roberts (September)
- Derek Clarkson: Crystalline Glazes (October)
- Potters: An exhibition to celebrate the 9th edition of *Potters*, the illustrated directory of the Craft Potters Association (November)
- Peter Beard 'New Ceramics' (November)

Showcases
John Calver (May) / Carol Wainwright (July) / Alan Heaps (September) / Sarah Robertson (October) / Fenella Mallalieu (November)

1993
- Clayworks III: Associate Members (February)
- Heart to Heart: Pots for Valentines (February)
- Robin Welch 'New Ceramics' (March)
- New Members: Keith Ashley, Bennett Cooper, Joanna Howells, Wendy Johnson, Hazel Johnston, Laurence McGowan, John Middlemiss, Lawson Oyekan, David White, Steve Woodhead (April)
- Jane Perryman (June)
- Ian Byers (July)
- Setting Out: Selected work by Art School Graduates '93 (August)
- Warren Mackenzie (October)
- Gabriele Koch (October)
- Ian Byers, Emmanuel Cooper, David Frith, Jane Hamlyn, Ruth King, John Maltby, Emily Myers, Phil Rogers, Ruthanne Tudball, David White 'Boxes' (November)

Showcases
Peter Clough (January) / Richard Phethean (March) / Bridget Drakeford (April) / Alan Heaps (May) / David Jones (May) / Chris Speyer (June) / Terri Holman (June) / Susan Nemeth (August) / John Higgins (September) / Gaynor Lindsell (October) / Paul Jackson

1994
- Fireworks2: Craft Potters Association Professionals (January)
- Karen Bunting, Jane Hamlyn, Alan Heaps, John Maltby, John Pollex, Nicola Werner 'Pots for Valentines' (February)

- Micki Schloessingk (May)
- Josie Walter (June)
- Aki Moriuchi and Sarah Jane-Selwood (July)
- Setting Out: Selected work by Art School Graduates (August)
- David Leach (September)
- Clive Bowen (October)
- Sebastian Blackie, Mick Casson, John Chalke, Rosette Gault, Janet Mansfield, Piet Stockmans 'Playing with Fire' (November)
- Ian Byers, Jack Doherty, Carolyn Genders, Ashley Howard, John Maltby, Sarah Monk, Tessa Wolfe Murray, John Wheeldon 'Candlesticks' (November)

Showcases

André Hess (May) / Nancy Pickard (June) / Sylph Baier (July) / Jacqueline Norris (September) / Nicola Werner (October) / Ursula Morley Price (November)

1995

- Clayworks IV (January)
- New Members: Peter Clough, John Higgins, Ashley Howard, Joanna Howells, Anne James, Marcio Mattos, Aki Moriuchi, Will Marshall (March)
- Ian Gregory (May)
- Ruthanne Tudball (June)
- Karen Bunting (June)
- Colin Pearson (July)
- Setting Out: Selected work by Art School Graduates (August)
- Duncan Ross (October)
- Tim Andrews, Linda Chew, Russell Coates, Bridget Drakeford, John Dunn, Andrew Hill, Will Marshall, Jacqueline Norris, John Wheeldon 'Glitter Christmas 1995'

Showcases

Pots for Valentines (February) / Sarah Monk (February) / Bernard Irwin (March) / Kochevet Ben-David (April) / Charles Spacey (May) / Mark Griffith (July)/ Richard Baxter (August) / Jo Connell (September) / Audrey Richardson (October) / John Berry (October) / Philomena Pretsell (November) / Janet Leach (November)

1996

- Fireworks III: Professional Members, including Susan Bruce, Rosemary Cochrane, Peter Hayes, André Hess, Sarah Monk and David White (January)
- Sheila Casson, Jack Doherty, Jane Hamlyn, Peter Meanley, Walter Keeler, Phil Rogers, Micki Schloessingk, Ruthanne Tudball and Sarah Walton 'Salt and Soda' (March)
- Phil Rogers (May)
- Nigel Lambert (June)
- Setting Out: Selected work by Art School Graduates (August)
- Jim Malone (September)
- Peter Lane (October)
- David Canter (October)

Showcases

Karin Hessenberg (February) / Vinitha McWhinnie (March) / David Brown (April) / Rosemary Cochrane (May) / Andy Lloyd (June) / Martin Booth (July) / Michael and Victoria Eden (August) / Christine Gittens (September) / Martin McWilliam (October) / Gaynor Reeve (November)

1997

- Stefanie Dinkelbach, Susan Halls, Emma Rodgers and Helen Talbot 'Prizewinners' (February)
- Kaleidoscope: A changing exhibition to celebrate the opening of the newly refurbished shop and gallery (May)
- Emily Myers (June)
- Loretta Braganza (July)
- Clive Bowen, Joanna Constantinidis, Walter Keeler, John Leech, David Roberts, Tim Andrews, Emmanuel Cooper, Edmund de Waal, David Jones, Gabriele Koch, David Leach, Lawrence McGowan, Jane Perryman 'Touching the Past' (September)
- Jane Hamlyn (October)
- Morgan Hall (November)

Showcases

Nick Membery (January) / Billy Adams (February) / S J Holliday (June) / Clare Conrad (June) / Jennifer Colquitt (July) / Gary Wood (August) / Billy Adams (September) / Susan Nemeth (October) / Steve Woodhead

1998

- Jack Doherty (May)
- Laurence McGowan (July)
- Jeff Oestreich (October)
- Jane Perryman (November)

Showcases

Maggie Williams (March) / Derek Emms (April) / Liz Gale (May) / Jonathan Garrett (June) / David Binns (July) / Steve Woodhead (August) / Gill Wright (September) / Maggie Berkowitz (October)

1999

- Setting Out '99: Selected work by Art School Graduates (January)
- Rupert Spira (March)
- Sasha Wardell (June)
- Anne James, Gabriele Koch, Gaynor Lindsell, Jane Perryman, Duncan Ross, Antonia Salmon, Tina Vlassopulos 'Burnt Earth' (July)
- John Higgins and André Hess (September)
- Kate Malone (October)
- Pots for Christmas (November)

Showcases

Gill Bliss (February) / Gilda Westermann (April) / Victoria Bryan (May) / Sotis Flippides (May) / Gareth Mason (July) / Robert Sanderson (August) / Hilary Roberts (August)

2000

- Setting Out 2000: Selected work by Art School Graduates (January)
- Peter Hayes (March)
- Joanna Howells (June)
- Clive Bowen, Richard Phethean, Mary Wandrausch, David Miller, Sean Miller, Josie Walter, Victoria and Michael Eden 'Slipware' (July)
- Nic Collins (September)
- David Frith (October)
- Emmanuel Cooper, Duncan Ross, Walter Keeler, Sasha Wardell, Emily Myers and Antonia Salmon 'Christmas Collection' (November)

Showcases
Sophie MacCarthy (February) / Val Cushing (May) / Nigel Lambert (June) / Sheila Casson (August) / John Jelfs (August) / Neil Brownsword (September)

2001

- Setting Out 2001: Selected work by Art School Graduates (January)
- Gill Bliss, Ian Gregory, Jude Jelfs, Christy Keeny, John Maltby, Sally MacDonell, Anne Kari Ramberg Marshall 'The Figure Show' (March)
- Tina Vlassopulos (May)
- Victoria Bryan, Sophie Cook, John Dawson, Karen Downing, Margaret Frith, Joanna Howels, David Jones, Peter Lane, Anne Kari Ramberg Marshall, Gareth Mason, Hilary Roberts, Sarah-Jane Selwood, Daniel Smith, Gilda Westermann 'Simple and Pure' (July)
- Linda Christianson (September)
- Richard Phethean (October)
- Paul Jackson (October)
- Jack Doherty (November)
- Jack Doherty, Aki Moriuchi, Peter Lane, Gareth Mason, Jane Hamlyn, Nigel Lambert 'Christmas Collection' (November)

Showcases
Michael Casson / Penny Fowler (May) / David Allnatt (June) / Les Rucinski (June) / Micki Scloessingk (September)

2002

- Setting Out: Selected work by Art School Graduates (January)
- Anna Lambert (March)
- Jack Doherty (April)
- Emily Myers (May)
- Aki Moriuchi (July)
- Walter Keeler (September)
- Duncan Ayscough, Joy Bosworth, Anne James, Emma Johnstone, Tony Laverick, Mary Rich, Caroline Whyman 'A Touch of Gold' (November)

Showcases
Sarah Walton (March) / Terry Bell-Hughes (April) / Gilles Le Corre (May) / Lisa Hammond (June) / Karen Bunting (June) / Claire Ireland (July) / Jane Cox (October) / Tim Hurn (September) / Martin Lungley (October)

2003

- Setting Out: Selected work by Art School Graduates (January)
- Mick Casson, Anne Kari Ramberg Marshall, Petra Reynolds, Micki Schloessingk and Ruthanne Tudball 'Tea Total' (March)
- Phil Rogers (May)
- Jane Perryman (June)
- Susan Nemeth (July)
- Jean-Nicolas Gerard (September)
- Sandy Brown (November)

Showcases
Peter Wills (April) / Ashraf Hanna (April) / Fiona Thompson (May) / Sarah Dunstan (July) / Petra Reynolds (August) / Jude Jelfs (September) / Susan Disley (October)

2004

- Setting Out 2004: Selected work by Art School Graduates (January)
- Micki Schloessingk (April)
- Terry Bell-Hughes, Victoria Bryan, Karen Bunting, Kyra Cane, Daphne Carnegy, Simon Carroll, Nic Collins, Susan Disley, Mike Dodd, Jack Doherty, Lisa Hammond, André Hess, Tim Hurn, Dan Kelly, Anja Lubach, Gareth Mason, Sean Miller, Aki Moriuchi, Richard Phethean, Nick Rees, Petra Reynolds, Sarah-Jane Selwod, Jeremy Steward, Gilda Westermann, Takeshi Yasuda 'Bloomers' (May)
- Martin McWilliam (June)
- Jim Malone (September)
- Gifted (November)

Showcases
Jitka Palmer (March) / Sean Miller (March) / Rob Sollis (April) / Jane Beeny (June) / Geraldine McGloin (July) / John Higgins (July) / Taja (August) / Anne James (September) / Chris Keenan (November) / Jeremy Steward (November)

2005

- Setting Out 2005: Selected work by Art School Graduates (February)
- Ray Finch, Peter Lane, David Leach, Eric Mellon, Ursula Mommens, Colin Pearson, Marianne de Trey, Rosemary D. Wren 'Celebration' (April)
- Mike Dodd (June)
- Ruthanne Tudball (July)
- Duncan Ross (September)
- Gifted (November)

Showcases
Anna Silverton (March) / Sophie Cook (April) / Julian Belmonte (May) / Christy Keeney (June) / Deirdre Burnett (August) / David Miller (September) / Duncan Hooson (October) / Peter Meanley (November)

2006

- Setting Out 2006: Selected work by Art School Graduates (January)
- Kochevet Bendavid, Daphne Carnegy, Nic Collins, Jack Doherty, Carolyn Genders, André Hess, John Higgins, Ashley Howard, Lisa Katzenstein, Anna Lambert, Nigel Lambert, Sophie MacCarthy, Gareth Mason, John Pollex, Petra Reynolds, Jeremy Steward, Taja, Josie Walter 'What a Dish!' (April)
- Ursula Mommens (July)
- Margaret Frith (September)
- Clive Bowen (November)

Showcases
Anja Lubach (February) / Prue Cooper (March) / Alasdair MacDonell (March) / Ian Gregory (June) / Wendy Hoare (July) / Tim Gee (August) / Marcus O'Mahony (September) / Carolyn Genders (October)

2007

- Setting Out 2007: Selected work by Art School Graduates (January)
- Kyra Cane, Susan Disley, Ashraf Hanna and Dan Kelly 'Monochrome' (March)
- Antonia Salmon (May)

Showcases
Craig Underhill (April) / Bruce Chivers (April) / Stephen Parry (June)

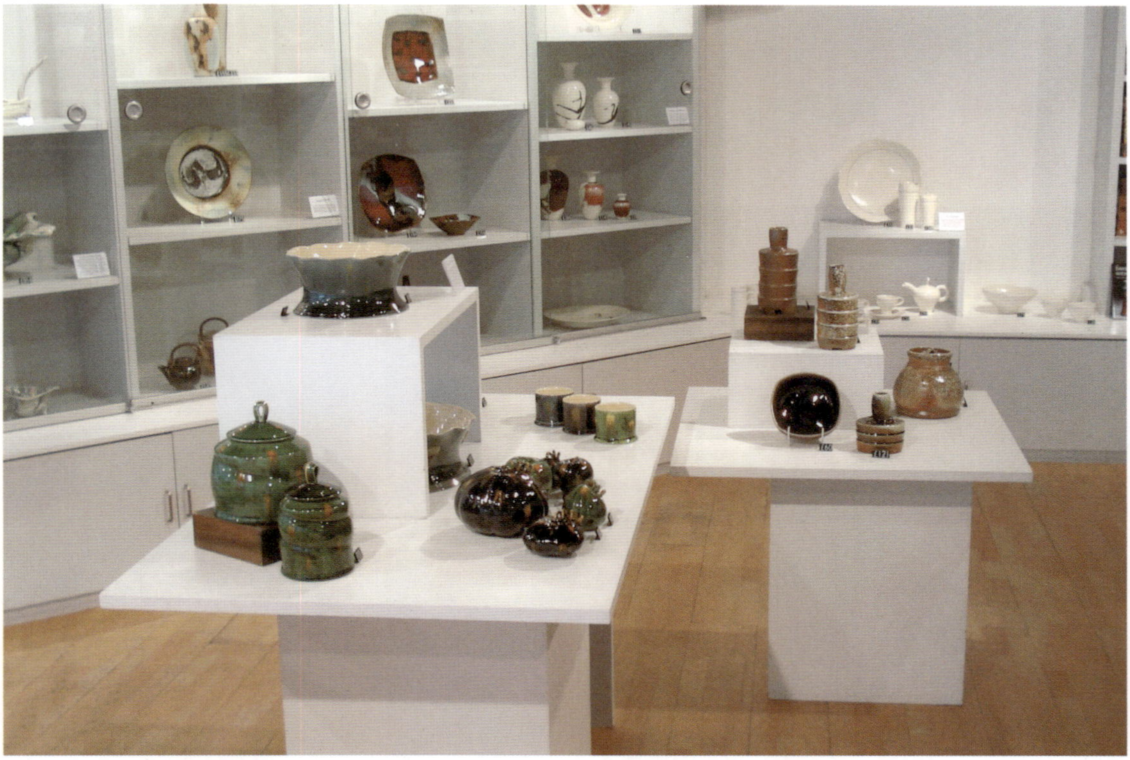

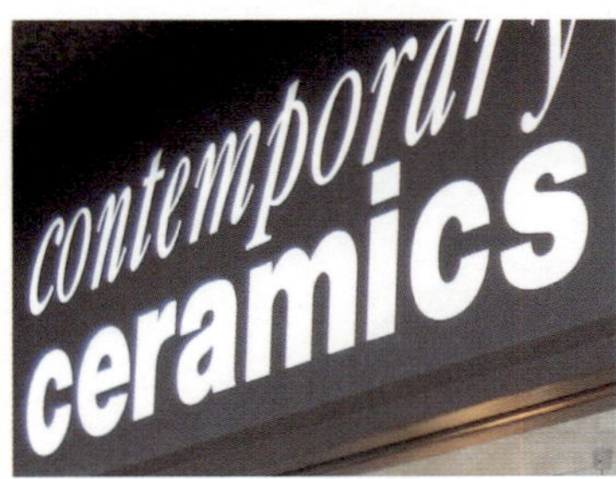
contemporary
ceramics

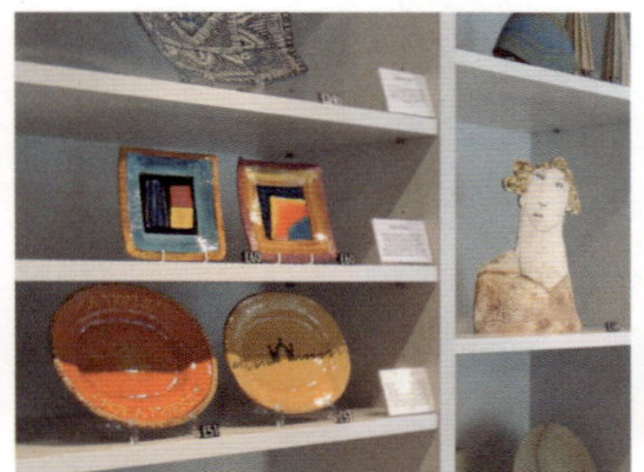

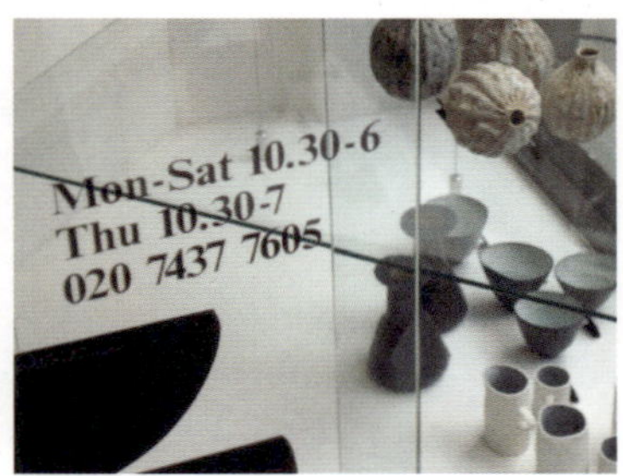
Mon-Sat 10.30-6
Thu 10.30-7
020 7437 7605

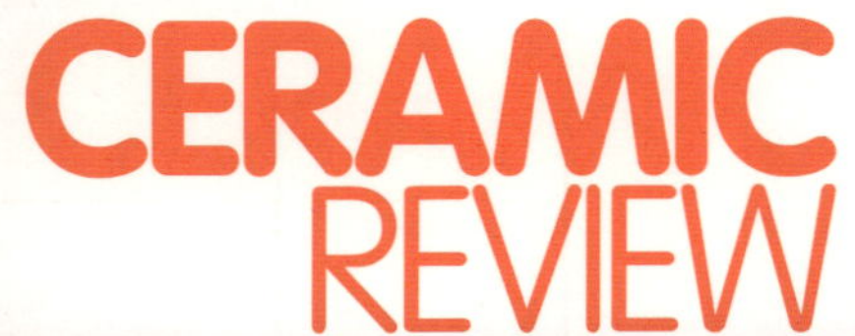

The Magazine of Ceramic Art and Craft
Issue 225 May/June 2007 £6.30
www.ceramicreview.com

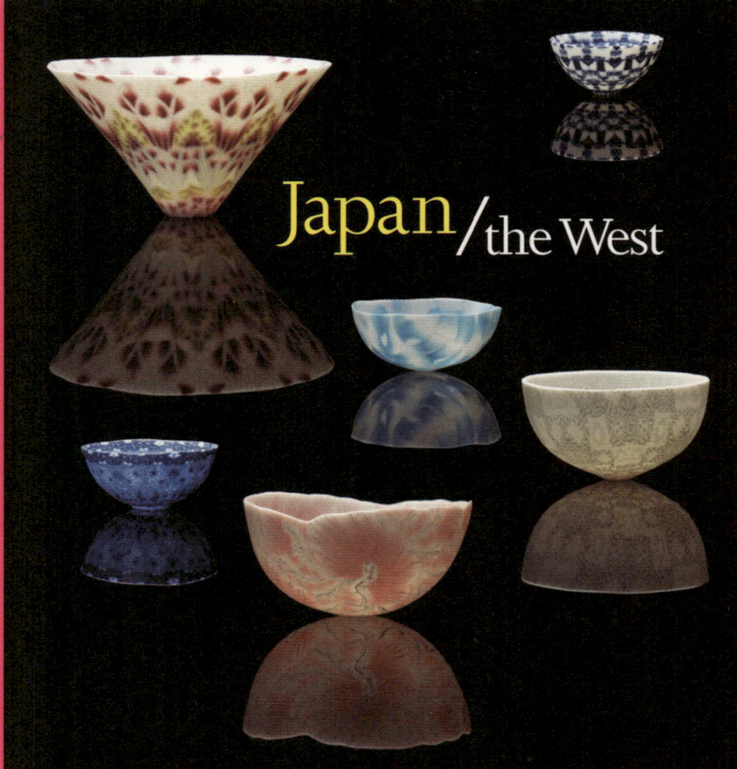

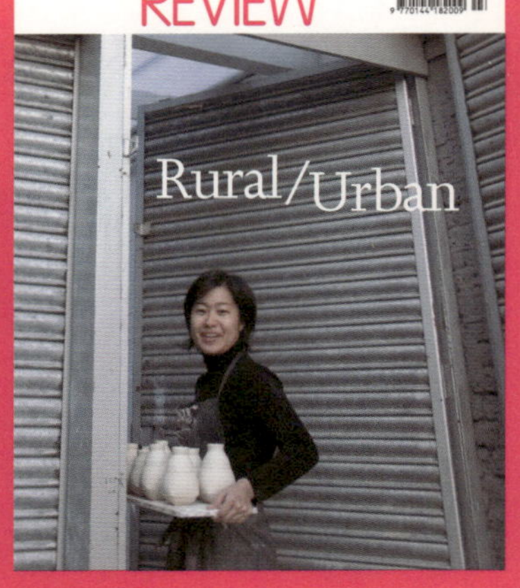

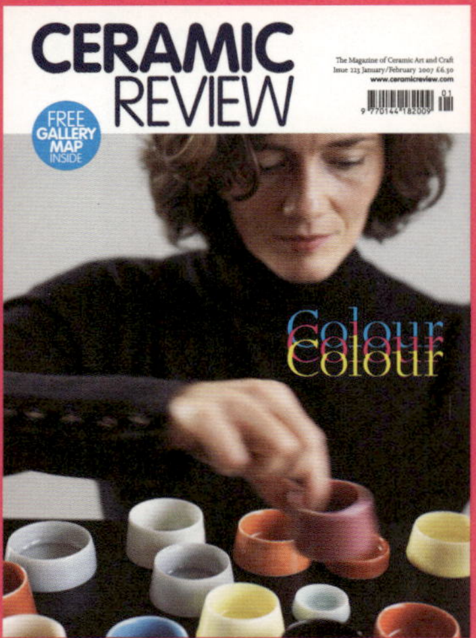